CONTENTS

INTRODUCTION 9

What Is Kamado Style Cooking? ... 9

How to Light the Char-Griller Kamado Grill ... 9

Using Your Char-Griller Kamado Grill ... 11

Cleaning out the Mold of Your Char-Griller Kamado Grill ... 12

FISH AND SEAFOOD ... 13

Grilled Shrimp Cocktail With Fire-roasted Cocktail Sauce ... 13

Grilled Salmon ... 13

Blue Cheese Compound Butter Grilled Oysters ... 14

Chicken And Shrimp Paella ... 14

Baked Brie With Chutney And Crisp Bacon ... 15

Blackened Grouper ... 15

Fish And Shrimp Stuffed Jalapeños ... 16

Grilled Shrimp And Linguica Skewers ... 16

Oysters On The Half Shell ... 17

Seared Scallops ... 17

Tuna Kabobs ... 18

Fish Tacos ... 18

Smoked Planked Trout ... 18

Swordfish Steaks With Peach Salsa ... 19

Oyster Spaghetti ... 19

Shrimp And Grits Kabobs ... 20

Scallops, Asparagus And Artichoke Gratin ... 21

Grilled Lobster ... 21

Foil Packet Fish Filets ... 22

Cold-smoked Rock Shrimp ... 22

Watermelon Pizza ... 22

Cajun Shrimp Burgers ... 23

Ginger Garlic Shrimp Stir-fry ... 24

Roasted Halibut With Greek Relish ... 24

Mediterranean Surf And Turf Kabobs ... 25

Bourbon-glazed Cold Smoked Salmon ... 25

Cedar Planked Honey Glazed Salmon With Grilled Lemon Butter Asparagus ... 26

Grilled Fish Tacos ... 27

Grilled Asian Mahi-mahi ... 27

Cigar Dave's Alpha-meal 28

Grilled Shrimp, Romaine And Avocado Salad 28

Cioppino (chip-ee-no) 28

Crab Quiche 29

POULTRY 30

Lemon Pepper Wings 30

Smoked Chicken Wings 30

Garfunkel Chicken 30

Grilled Duck Breast With Apple Brandy Glaze 31

Champagne Quail 32

Smoked Wings With Moonshine White Sauce And Ranch Pickles 32

Bacon-wrapped Bbq Quail 32

Lemon Scented Chicken Thighs 33

O'neill Williams' Turkey Parmesan 33

Cuban Chicken Bombs 33

Hatch Chile Salsa And Chicken Casserole 34

Barbecue Chicken With Alabama White Sauce 34

Vidalia Onion And Sriracha-glazed Nashville Hot Wings 35

Rosemary Grilled Chicken Sandwiches 36

Polynesian Duck Kabobs 36

Open-faced Leftover Turkey Sandwich 37

Smoky Thai Pulled Chicken Sandwiches 37

Hop's Hawaiian Bbq Chicken Pizza 38

Brined Roasted Turkey 39

Whole Smoked Barbecue Chicken 39

Smoky Grilled Chicken Nachos 40

Lamb Shawarma 40

Savory Beer Can Chicken 41

Grilled Chicken Fajita Skewers 41

Greg Bates Bbq Chicken 42

Amusement Park Turkey Legs 42

Grill Glazed Sweet Asian Chicken Pan Grill 43

Bou Lentil Turkey Burgers 43

Chicken & Dumplings 44

Wild Rice Turkey Biryani Stuffed Whole Pumpkin 44

Hoisin Glazed Wings 45

Peking Duck 45

Country Chicken Saltimbocca 46

DESSERTS 48

Grilled Plums With Honey And Ricotta 48

Brownies 48

Caramel Cinnamon Rolls 48

Upside Down Triple Berry Pie 49

Berry Upside-down Cake 49

Grilled Sopapillas 50

4 Ingredient, No Knead Bread 50

Death By Chocolate 51

3 Ingredient Fruit Cobbler 51

Chocolate Cake 51

Peach Dutch Baby 52

Fresh Peach Crisp 53

Chocolate Chip Cookie Peanut Butter Cup S'mores 53

Apple Pizza 53

Orange Scented Vanilla Cake 53

Grilled Watermelon With Honey Yogurt 54

Grilled Pineapple Sundaes 54

Best Banana Bread 54

Peaches And Pound Cake 55

Triple Berry Crostata 55

Almond Cream Cake 56

Whole Apples With Caramel Sauce 56

Peanut Butter Bacon Bars 57

Banana Boats 57

S'mores Pizza 57

Sourdough Baguette 58

Buttermilk Biscuits 59

Corn & Jalapeño Focaccia 59

Seasonal Fruit Cobbler 60

Lemon Poppy Seed Cake 60

Grilled Naan 61

Pizza Margherita 61

Nutella And Strawberry Pizza 62

BEEF 63

Cranberry-marinated Rack Of Lamb 63

Brisket Burnt Ends 63

Aged Prime Rib 64

Smoked Beef Short Ribs...65

Fire Grilled Steak With Steakhouse Butter.....................................66

Smoked Beef Birria 66

Asian Beef & Mushroom Tacos 67

Smoked Oxtail Stew 67

Red Gold Spicy Burgers 68

Seared Bison Filet..68

Grilled Top Blade Steak 68

Bacon Cheeseburger Hotdogs 69

Short Ribs & Polenta 70

Ray's At Killer Creek's Short Ribs..71

Steakhouse Meatballs With French Fries And Tzatziki Sauce 71

Korean-style Beef Short Ribs 72

Beef Asparagus Stir Fry 72

Smoked Beef Brisket 73

Round Roast Cheesesteaks With Pepper Jack Cheese Sauce 73

London Bridge London Broil...74

Pulled Lamb Nachos 74

Ultimate Bacon Jam Burger 75

Ny Strip Steaks..75

Pastrami Beef Short Ribs..76

Smoked Bourbon Chili...77

Stir-fry Szechuan Beef..77

Ray's Herb Butter Prime Rib 78

Reverse-sear Ribeye 78

Taco Soup 79

Grilled Buffalo Steaks..79

Pimento Cheese Burger With Bacon Jam 80

Herbed-up Prime Rib 80

Korean Short Ribs 81

BURGERS 82

Breakfast Burger 82

Classic American Burger 82

Oahu Burger 83

Quesadilla Burger 83

The Crowned Jewels Burger 83

"the Masterpiece" 84

PORK...85

Reuben Riffel's Yellow Bellied Pork 85

Smoked Pork Loin Sandwich 85

Bacon Roses 86

Chile Rubbed Grilled Pork Chops 87

Fresh Smoked Bacon 87

Stir-fried Cucumber And Pork With Golden Garlic 88

Championship Ribs 88

Baby Back Ribs With Quince Barbecue Sauce 89

Bacon Mac & Cheese 90

Porchetta 91

Smoked Andouille & Crawfish Gumbo 91

Brunswick Stew 92

Adobo Chicken Wings 93

Prosciutto Wrapped Cheese Dogs 94

Honey Pork Tenderloin Kabob 94

Country Christmas 94

Cuban Pork (lechon Asado) 96

Sriracha Pork Chops 96

Famous Dave's Five Star Bbq Sticky Ribs 97

Chili Crusted Boar Ham 98

Beer-infused Baby Back Ribs 98

Pig Candy 99

Spicy Bbq Spare Ribs 99

Braised Carnitas With Chimichurri Sauce 100

Carolina Pulled Pork 101

Herb-crusted Pork Short Ribs 102

Apple Cinnamon Pork Chops 102

Charlotte Pork Chops 103

Pork Cacciatore 103

Stuffed Pork Chops With Poblano Cream Sauce 104

Takeo Spikes' Ribs 104

Pineapple-glazed Kurobuta Bone-in Ham With Bourbon-cherry Sauce 105

SIDES **107**

Corn, Bacon & Chorizo Hash 107

Cheesy Tomato Risotto 107

Panzanella 108

Grilled Artichokes 108

Potato, Squash, And Tomato Gratin 108

Roasted Potatoes 109

Dutch Oven Baked Beans 109

Ratatouille 110

Broiled Tomatoes And Parmesan...110

Grilled Watermelon Salad 110

Grilled Lemon Garlic Zucchini 111

Wood-plank Loaded Mashed Potatoes 111

Smoked Potato Salad..112

Corn & Tomato Salsa 112

Grilled Caesar Salad 113

Sweet Potato Bake 113

Corn & Poblano Pudding..114

Prosciutto And Pear Bruschetta 114

Mexican Street Corn 114

Soba Noodle Bowl 115

Baba Ganoush 115

Cowboy Caviar 116

Summer Squash & Eggplant 116

Campfire Potato Salad 117

Sweet Potato Fries 117

Mac And Cheese 117

Wood-plank Stuffed Tomatoes 118

Alligator Eggs 118

German Potato Salad 119

Grilled Paneer 119

RECIPE INDEX.. 121

INTRODUCTION

What Is Kamado Style Cooking?

A Kamado grill allows you to cook food fast and hot, or low and slow, over burning charcoal embers. You can even toss some of our exceptionally flavored wood pellets into your Kamado grill to give ingredients authentic, one-of-a-kind tastes like apple, pecan and hickory.

Although you might have used a more traditional, lower end charcoal grill in the past, a Kamado style grill allows you to more conveniently balance your target temperatures. Plus, you can cook a lot of food at once in a relatively small footprint.

Kamado grill cooking provides a wonderful way to cook almost anything you want.

How to Light the Char-Griller Kamado Grill

One of the best things about Kamado grills is they allow for over-the-fire cooking.

You get to mold your coals, stack them delicately, and keep the embers going while you cook your meat.

This comes with its own challenges though, and it can be a skill learning how to keep the temperature of your fire at just the right levels for good Kamado cooking.

Just like with charcoal grilling, Kamado grilling can be done either directly over a hot fire, or as low and slow smoking.

Both are great barbecue methods that are specific to different types of cooking, but they each require very different setups. Knowing how to do both will make sure you master kamado cooking quickly.

Direct grilling is exactly what it sounds like. It's grilling your food directly over the fire. It's perfect for creating beautifully seared meat and grill marks, and for simple BBQ food like hamburgers and hot dogs. The problem with direct grilling is that it's perfect for meat that only needs short blasts of heat to cook it. In some instances though, we need something lower and slower that cooks meat without exposing it to ridiculous temperatures.

This is where indirect grilling comes in. Often also called 2-zone cooking, it involves setting up two heat zones across your grilling surface.

The first zone sits over your fire, but with no food on it. The other zone is where you put your meat, but with no heat directly beneath it. This setup allows the heat from your fire to create ambient heat, much like you would have in an oven, which in turn cooks your meat.

What makes this different to direct grilling is that it doesn't expose your meat to high temperatures. This allows it to retain its juices without the skin to drying out or burning.

To set up for indirect grilling, drop a generous amount of coal into the main chamber of your grill. Arrange the coals into a rough peak, and place fire-starters in the pile about one-third down. Don't use lighter fluid.

Charcoal can take a while to reach your target temperature, so place the lid on your grill and allow the coals to heat up. Usually this takes about 10-15 minutes, but measure the internal temperature of your grill with a thermometer. You also want your coals to have settled down a bit, and in the form of embers rather than raging flames.

This kind of approach to lighting is called top-down because it's just that: Your fire is lit by starting at the top of the fire and burns downwards. The reason this works is because it tends to last for longer (sometimes for as long as 10-12 hours) before you need to start replenishing your coals. This is especially true in kamado grills because the insulation is so good.

Once the grill is ready, add your smoking stone insert (this usually comes with your kamado grill), which works by effectively diverting heat away from your heat. Don't forget to insert your grill grate.

Allow a few more minutes for the fire to stabilize (any opening of the grill's lid will disturb the temperature in your grill) before then adding your food to the indirect zone of your grill.

Direct grilling setup is far more straightforward, and is much the same as regular charcoal grilling.

With direct grilling it's ok to be a bit looser with coal formation, so I tend to get them going in a charcoal chimney before then transferring to the grill chamber. No need for top-down. We just want a good amount of coal on the go as quickly as possible.

Put a generous amount of coals in the chamber and insert several fire-starters across them. We want high heat quickly.

Shut the lid and allow the grill temperature to reach your target temperature before inserting your grill and placing your food on the surface.

Using Your Char-Griller Kamado Grill

1. Adding Charcoal to Your Char-Griller Kamado Grill

Start with a clean, empty firebox.

Stack charcoal into the firebox. You can use either lump charcoal or briquettes. To stop any smaller pieces falling down and obstructing the airflow, make sure you stack them right on the fire grate, ensuring that the larger pieces are on the bottom.

Put the smaller lump pieces on top. You can use leftover lumps from a previous smoke if you have some. There is no need to fill up the entire firebox. How much you put in will depend on the length of the cook. Finding how long your charcoal will last will take some experimenting.

2. Firing up Your Char-Griller Kamado Grill

Fully open both the top and bottom vent.

Make a small "well" in the middle of the pile of coals. Place your fire starter in the well, and light it. Leave it to light up fully.

Once the fire starter is burning well, place some of the larger lumps of charcoal on top of the fire starter. Wait for some of the lumps to light up.

Once the fire is established, add in any accessories and racks that you will need for your cook.

3. Adjusting the Vents

Close the lid, leaving the vents fully open.

Watch your thermometer. Once the temperature has reached about 100°F below your target temperature, start shutting the vents. You will need to experiment a little, but generally leaving the top vent open a crack, and shutting the bottom vent to around 50% will slow the fire enough.

Keep monitoring the temperature. As you get closer to the target, shut the vents down some more.

As you get closer to the target temperature, you will find it easier to make final adjustments by using the top vent only.

4. Reaching Your Target Temperature

At this point it might also be a good idea to start monitoring the temperature using a digital thermometer, as they are more accurate. If you have reached temperature, but it is still rising, then you will need to shut the top vent down some more.

Once the temperature has stopped at your desired temperature, you have no need to touch your vents. The temperature will remain stable over the duration of the cook.

Cleaning out the Mold of Your Char-Griller Kamado Grill

Yep, this one's a bit more gruesome. But for anyone who's experienced mold turning up in their bathroom or kitchen, they'll attest to the importance of nipping this stuff in the bud the moment if threatens to rear its ugly head.

It's not uncommon to go a few months without using your grill, especially over the winter months. Unfortunately this can mean that in that time sheltered away, mold can start to gather inside the grill. This is especially problematic if it turns up on the grilling grates or in the internal walls of the chamber.

If this happens – don't worry. It's very common, and is very easy to get rid of in a kamado grill and be done entirely without the use of any cleaning chemicals.

Here's how to do it:

1. Heat up your grill and place all components like the grilling grates and heat deflectors in the grill where they normally fit.

2. Open the grill dampers/vents up fully and close the kamado lid. Leave the grill and ramp the temperature right up high, to about 500-600°F. Don't go higher than this as it can put undue stress on your grill.

3. When the grill reaches this temperature range (use a temperature gauge to check), keep it at this heat for about 20 minutes. Then, close the intake damper (the bottom vent) and let it cook for a further 20 minutes. Then close the exhaust damper (top vent).

4. With the vents shut, the heat in the grill will naturally die down. Allow the grill to cool down completely.

5. Once the grill has cooled, open it and use a grill brush to clean the grates. You can do this without soapy water or chemicals.

This method can take a little bit of time, but is a fantastic way to do away with any unwanted dirt or mold naturally and – crucially – without the use of any chemical agents, so you don't run the risk of contaminating your food or leaving any traces of nasty smells or tastes.

FISH AND SEAFOOD

Grilled Shrimp Cocktail With Fire-roasted Cocktail Sauce

Servings:4
Cooking Time: 35 Minutes

Ingredients:
- 1 tablespoon olive oil
- 1/2 teaspoon Garlic Salt
- 16 jumbo shrimp (about 1 pound), peeled and deveined 1 cup Fire-Roasted Cocktail Sauce
- 1 tablespoon chopped flat-leaf (Italian) parsley
- 1 lemon, cut into 4 wedges or 8 slices
- 1 cup canned no-salt-added fire-roasted diced tomatoes
- 1 tablespoon horseradish
- 1 tablespoon lime juice
- 1/4 teaspoon Chipotle Puree (optional)

Directions:
1. Preheat the grill to 350°F using direct heat with a cast iron grate installed.
2. Combine the oil and garlic salt in a medium bowl. Add the shrimp and toss well.
3. Skewer the shrimp, place the shrimp on the cooking grid and cook for about 3 minutes on each side, or until pink and firm. Remove from the heat.
4. Spoon 1/4 cup of cocktail sauce into each of 4 decorative glasses. Top with 4 shrimp per glass. Sprinkle with the parsley and garnish with the lemon wedges or slices.
5. Combine all the ingredients in a blender or food processor and puree until smooth. Transfer the sauce to a jar and chill for at least 30 minutes before using to let the flavors meld. The sauce will keep in the refrigerator for about 1 month.

Grilled Salmon

Servings:4
Cooking Time: 30 Minutes

Ingredients:
- Salmon fillets (with skin on), 4 to 5 ounces per serving
- 1/2 cup soy sauce
- 1/2 cup lemon juice
- 1/3 cup brown sugar, packed
- 1/4 cup vegetable oil
- 2 cloves garlic, crushed
- 2 tbsp butter, melted
- 2 tbsp maple syrup
- Your favorite commercial or homemade dry BBQ rub, to taste

Directions:
1. Combine soy sauce, lemon juice, brown sugar, oil and garlic and stir to dissolve sugar. Pour into a zippered-top plastic bag and add salmon. Marinate in the refrigerator for 3 to 6 hours.
2. After marinating, allow the salmon to stand at room temperature for 30 minutes before grilling, then pat dry with a paper towel.
3. Mix together the butter and maple syrup and brush over entire surface of the salmon. Sprinkle with a liberal amount of BBQ rub.
4. Preheat the grill to 350°F using direct heat with a cast iron grate installed, place the salmon on a fish grid and cook for 15 to 20 minutes. Salmon is done when a knife inserted in the fillet slides in easily with no resistance and flesh is no longer opaque.

5. Remove salmon; using a clean brush, brush on any remaining maple syrup/butter mixture and wrap in foil for 5 to 10 minutes before serving.

Blue Cheese Compound Butter Grilled Oysters

Servings:6
Cooking Time: 4 Minutes

Ingredients:
- ½ bushel of oysters, appx. 50
- 12 strips of bacon, cooked and chopped
- 1 lb. unsalted butter
- 4 oz. crumbled blue cheese
- 1 tbsp garlic powder
- 1 tbsp minced celery leaves
- 1 tbsp minced chives
- 2 tsp hot sauce
- 1 zest of lemon
- Salt to taste

Directions:
1. Preheat the grill to 300°F using direct heat with a cast iron grate installed.
2. Clean and detach the oysters from the shell. Place a bit of the butter mixture on top of each oyster; the compound butter recipe should be enough for the half bushel.
3. Place the oysters on a Perforated Cooking Grid; cook for 3 to 4 minutes or until the butter has melted.
4. Mix all the ingredients for the compound butter together and set aside.

Chicken And Shrimp Paella

Servings:6
Cooking Time: 30 Minutes

Ingredients:
- 15 large shrimp (feel free to add clams or mussels)
- 1 lb (450 g) chicken thighs
- 8 cups (1.9 L) chicken stock
- 1 pinch saffron
- ½ cup (120 ml) fresh parsley
- 2 to 3 tbsp (30 to 45 ml) fresh thyme
- 8 oz (225 g) chorizo sausages, sliced bite-size
- 3 garlic cloves, minced
- 1 large onion, diced
- 1 large bell pepper, diced
- 4 plum tomatoes, diced
- 4 tbsp (60 ml) tomato paste
- ½ tbsp (8 ml) paprika
- 1 cup (240 ml) olives, pitted and diced
- 3 cups (710 ml) calasparra rice
- 3 lemons, quartered

Directions:
1. Preheat the grill to 500°F using direct heat with a cast iron grate installed.
2. Peel shrimp, leaving on the tail. Lightly salt the chicken thighs and shrimp. Heat the chicken stock with saffron and herbs; keep hot but not boiling as you cook.
3. Coat the bottom of a Stir-Fry & Paella Pan with olive oil. Add the pan to the cooking grid and brown the chorizo for 1 or 2 minutes; set aside. Brown the chicken for 2 to 3 minutes; set aside.
4. Sauté garlic, onion and bell pepper until softened, adding tomatoes shortly before the mixture is finished. Add the tomato paste, paprika and olives; stir in the chicken and chorizo. Add rice, mixing together and stirring one minute. When the rice is slightly translucent add enough chicken stock to cover the whole mixture and lower the kamado grill temperature to 375°F.

5. Stir a few times in the first 10 minutes, adding broth as necessary to keep the rice fully covered. After this let the paella sit and cook another 10-20 minutes, adding broth bit by bit to keep the rice submerged until the rice on the top is al dente. Stir the paella one last time and place the shrimp on top, turning over after 2 to 4 minutes to cook on the other side. Carefully remove the paella from the kamado grill, cover and let rest for 15-20 minutes. Garnish with lemon wedges.

Baked Brie With Chutney And Crisp Bacon

Servings:8
Cooking Time: 65 Minutes

Ingredients:

- 1 large Granny Smith apple, diced
- 1 medium onion, diced
- 1/2 red bell pepper, chopped
- 1/2 cup sugar
- 1/3 cup cider vinegar
- 1/4 cup water
- 1 tablespoon balsamic vinegar
- 1 tablespoon minced garlic
- 3/4 cup chopped dried apricots
- 1/2 cup raisins
- 2 teaspoons grated peeled fresh ginger
- 1 1/2 teaspoons mustard seeds
- 1/4 teaspoons mustard seeds
- 1/4 teaspoon cayenne
- 1/4 teaspoon salt
- One 16-ounce round Brie
- 12 slices bacon, cooked crisp and chopped
- Crusty bread or crackers, for serving

Directions:

1. To make the chutney, in a Stir-Fry & Paella Pan on the kamado grill, or a large saucepan over medium- high heat on the stove top, combine the apple, onion, pepper, sugar, cider vinegar, water, balsamic vinegar, and garlic. Bring to a boil and reduce to a low simmer. Cook for 15 minutes, and continue cooking until the mixture thickens slightly and becomes syrupy, about 35 minutes. Remove from the heat and cool. This can be made the day ahead and refrigerated.

2. Preheat the grill to 350°F using direct heat with a cast iron grate installed. Place the Brie on a Baking Stone or an aluminum-foil pan. Heap the chutney over and around the Brie. Cook, covered, for 15 minutes, or until the Brie begins to melt. Top with the chopped bacon. Serve with crusty bread or crackers.

Blackened Grouper

Servings:2
Cooking Time: 10 Minutes

Ingredients:

- Grouper (thick is best)
- Chef Paul Prudhomme's blackening seasoning
- Butter

Directions:

1. Preheat the grill to 500°F using direct heat with a cast iron grate installed.

2. Season grouper with seasoning.

3. Add butter to the griddle, followed by the grouper.

4. Cook for three minutes, flip grouper and cook for another three minutes.

5. Remove grouper from kamado grill and place on plate on top of cheese grits.

Fish And Shrimp Stuffed Jalapeños

Servings:6
Cooking Time: 15 Minutes

Ingredients:

- Grouper
- 1 pound jalapenos
- 4-6 oz cream cheese
- 1-2 pounds shrimp
- 1 pound bacon
- Seasoning

Directions:

1. Preheat the grill to 400°F using direct heat with a cast iron grate installed.

2. Cook the grouper on a Perforated Cooking Grid. Mix with cream cheese when cooked.

3. Cut the stems off and split the jalapenos in half long ways. Use your knife to cut out the vein through the middle of the jalapeno with all the seeds. If you do not remove the seeds, your peppers will be very spicy. After removing the seeds, place the hollowed out jalapenos into your strainer and rinse them thoroughly.

4. Fill the hollowed out peppers with cream cheese and grouper. Remove the tail from your shrimp and place a single piece on top of your jalapeno. Wrap your jalapeno with half a slice of bacon and set into a Deep Dish Baking Stone.

5. Once all the jalapenos are wrapped, sprinkle with seasoning. Place jalapenos on the kamado grill for 15 minutes turning them half way through.

Grilled Shrimp And Linguica Skewers

Servings:4
Cooking Time: 18 Minutes

Ingredients:

- 2 each large Roma tomatoes
- 3 garlic cloves, roasted
- 1 tsp. salt
- ½ tsp. smoked paprika
- ¼ lb. unsalted butter, softened
- 2 tbsp. sherry vinegar
- 1 cup chopped fresh herbs (basil, parsley, cilantro, oregano)
- 1 tbsp. chopped capers
- 1 tsp. reserved juice from capers
- ½ tsp. lemon juice
- ¼ tsp. chili flakes
- 1 garlic clove, minced
- ¼ cup extra virgin olive oil
- 4 – 12" bamboo or metal skewers (bamboo soak in water for at least an hour)
- 16 each wild caught shrimp, U/12 size, head off, tail on, peeled and deveined
- 16 slices Linguica Sausage, ½"- ¾" thick
- 2 tbsp. blended olive oil or canola oil
- 4 tbsp. smoked tomato butter
- 2 tbsp. herb salsa verde
- Salt and pepper to taste

Directions:

1. Preheat the grill to 225°F using direct heat with a cast iron grate installed.

2. Cut the tomatoes in half; add to the grid and smoke tomatoes for 10 minutes until they are tender; set aside to cool.

3. Using a mortar and pestle or food processor, grind or process the roasted garlic, salt, smoked paprika and sherry vinegar into a paste. Mix the combination with the softened butter, and then grind the tomatoes together with the butter.

4. In a mixing bowl, combine all ingredients together and mix.

5. Preheat the grill to 375°F using direct heat with a cast iron grate installed.

6. Place a slice of Linguica sausage in the center of the shrimp; the shrimp will curl around the coin of sausage. Poke the skewer through the top of the shrimp, through the sausage and into the other end of the shrimp. The shrimp and sausage need to hold tightly on the skewer. Continue to complete the skewers, 2-3 shrimp and Linguica slices per skewer.

7. Brush the shrimp skewers lightly with oil and season with salt and pepper. Grill the skewers for approximately 6 minutes, turning them halfway through for desired grill markings and even cooking. Brush the skewers with the soft smoked tomato butter. Close the lid and cook for approximately 2 minutes.

8. With tongs, remove the skewers from the grill and spoon the herb salsa verde over the skewers.

Oysters On The Half Shell

Servings: 4

Cooking Time: 9 Minutes

Ingredients:

- 16 whole oysters
- 1/2 cup butter, softened
- 2 Tablespoons fresh parsley
- 2 cloves garlic, minced
- The zest of 1 lemon

Directions:

1. In a small bowl, combine butter, parsley, garlic, and lemon zest. Set aside

2. Grilling:

3. Preheat the grill to 425°F using direct heat with a cast iron grate installed.

4. Place the cleaned oysters, cup side down, directly on the grids and close the dome for 7-9 minutes or until the oysters open up.

5. Remove the top shells and spoon in equal portions of the compound butter. Close the dome for 1 minute more until the butter melts and serve.

Seared Scallops

Servings: 8

Cooking Time: 25 Minutes

Ingredients:

- 2 tbsp olive oil
- 1 tbsp unsalted butter
- 24 sea scallops, U-10
- kosher salt and freshly ground white pepper
- for the beurre blanc
- 1/2 cup white wine
- 1 tsp ground black pepper
- 4 sprigs of fresh thyme
- 1/4 cup rice wine vinegar
- 1 cup fresh raspberries
- 1 shallot, minced
- 1/2 cup heavy cream
- 1/2 cup cold unsalted butter, cut into cubes
- 1 tbsp soy sauce, plus more as desired

Directions:

1. To make the beurre blanc, in a medium saucepan, combine wine, pepper, thyme, vinegar, raspberries, and shallot, and place on the stovetop over medium heat. Simmer until reduced to a thin layer of liquid on the bottom of the pot, about 10 minutes. Add cream, and reduce until it has cooked down to a thin layer again, about 5 to 7 minutes. Slowly add butter, stirring constantly. Taste and season with salt, pepper, and soy sauce.

2. Preheat the grill to 500°F (260°C) using direct heat with a cast iron griddle installed. Add

oil and butter to the griddle. Once butter has melted, place scallops on the griddle, close the lid, and sear until brown on top and bottom, about 2 to 4 minutes each side.

3. Remove scallops from the grill and divide evenly among serving plates. Spoon warm beurre blanc over top. Serve immediately.

Tuna Kabobs

Servings:2
Cooking Time: 10 Minutes

Ingredients:
- 2 tuna steaks, cut into 2-inch pieces
- 1 large red bell pepper, cut into 2-inch pieces
- 1 sweet onion, cut into 2-inch pieces
- 1 pineapple, cut into 2-inch pieces
- 1 cup Sweet Kentucky Bourbon Grilling Glaze
- Salt and pepper to taste

Directions:
1. Preheat the grill to 350°F using direct heat with a cast iron grate installed.
2. Thread the tuna, red bell peppers, onion and pineapple onto the skewers, leaving a small space between each item. Salt and pepper to taste.
3. Grill for 5 minutes then brush on the Sweet Kentucky Bourbon Grilling Glaze on both sides. Grill for another 5 minutes; glaze once more and remove from the kamado grill. Let rest for 10 minutes. Enjoy!

Fish Tacos

Servings:8
Cooking Time: 10 Minutes

Ingredients:
- 4 tilapia filets
- 1 cup bell pepper (green, red, orange or assorted), sliced into strips
- ½ onion, sliced into strips
- Dizzy Pig Seasoning
- Olive oil
- Cilantro
- 8 tortillas
- Optional: lettuce, cheese, salsa

Directions:
1. Preheat the grill to 350°F using direct heat with a cast iron grate installed. Preheat Half Moon Cast Iron Griddle on the cooking grid.
2. Toss fish in olive oil and sprinkle liberally with seasoning.
3. Add the peppers and onions to the ridged side of the Griddle. Cook for 5 minutes. Add fish fillets to the cooking grid or a Half Moon Perforated Cooking Grid and cook for 5 minutes. Turn and cook until opaque.
4. Remove from the kamado grill and assemble with your favorite taco toppings.

Smoked Planked Trout

Servings:4
Cooking Time: 25 Minutes

Ingredients:
- 4 whole trout (12 to 16 ounces each)
- Sea salt and freshly ground black pepper
- 16 whole fresh basil leaves
- 1 lemon, thinly sliced and seeded, plus 4 half lemons for smoking and serving
- 2 tablespoons cold unsalted butter, thinly sliced
- 8 thin slices pancetta or prosciutto

Directions:
1. Preheat the grill to 450°F using direct heat with a cast iron grate installed. Grill the planks

until lightly singed on both sides, 2 minutes per side. Let cool.

2. Rinse the trout, inside and out, under cold running water, then blot dry, inside and out, with paper towels. Generously season the trout inside and out with salt and pepper. Place 3 to 4 basil leaves, lemon slices, and butter slices in the cavity of each trout.

3. Tie two pieces of pancetta to each trout, one on top, one on the bottom, using 3 pieces of butchers' string to secure them. Arrange the trout on the grilling planks and place a half lemon on each plank.

4. Meanwhile, adjust the vents on your grill to reduce the temperature to 350°F. (Less air means lower temperatures.) Arrange the planks on the kamado grill grid.

5. Smoke-roast the trout until the pancetta is sizzling and crisp and the trout is cooked through (140°F in the center), 15 to 20 minutes at 350°F.

6. Serve the trout on the planks with the smoked lemons for squeezing.

Swordfish Steaks With Peach Salsa

Servings: 4
Cooking Time: 15 Minutes

Ingredients:

- 4 swordfish steaks (about 1 inch thick, or 6 ounces)
- 1 Tablespoon olive oil
- Salt & Pepper
- 1/4 cup finely diced red pell pepper
- 1 Tablespoon olive oil
- 1/4 tsp cumin
- 2 peaches, slightly underripe, diced
- 1 jalapeño, seeded and finely chopped
- The juice and zest of 1 lime

Directions:

1. Combine ingredients for the salsa and set aside.

2. Brush both sides of the swordfish steaks with olive oil and season with salt and pepper.

3. Grilling:

4. Preheat the grill to 400°F using direct heat with a cast iron grate installed.

5. Place the steaks directly on the grid and close the dome for 6 minutes.

6. Gently flip the fish and close the dome for another 6-8 minutes or until the fish is firm.

7. Remove from the grid and serve topped with peach salsa.

Oyster Spaghetti

Servings:6
Cooking Time: 15 Minutes

Ingredients:

- 2 Tablespoons salted butter
- ½ cup diced shallots
- ¼ cup finely chopped green onions (white and green parts)
- 3 Tablespoons chopped garlic
- 1 cup vermouth (or white wine)
- 1½ cups Oyster Liquor
- 3 cups heavy cream
- 1 bay leaf
- 1 tablespoon chopped fresh thyme
- 48 large Gulf oysters, shucked
- 1 pound cooked spaghetti
- ½ cup grated Parmesan cheese
- Salt and freshly ground white pepper to taste
- Optional garnishes (shaved parmesan leaves, grated bottarga)

Directions:

1. Preheat the grill to 450°F using direct heat with a cast iron grate installed. Melt the salted

butter. Sauté the shallots and green onions for 3 minutes or until translucent. Reduce the heat to 375°F. Add the garlic and and sauté for 1 minute more. Add the vermouth, swirl the pan to deglaze, and allow the mixture to simmer for 2 minutes. Add the oyster liquor, heavy cream, bay leaf and fresh thyme and simmer all ingredients for 8 to 10 minutes, until the cream is bubbling and the sauce begins to reduce. Stir in the parmesan cheese.

2. Add the oysters and cook until the edges begin to curl. Season with salt and white pepper. Add the cooked spaghetti, and cook until pasta is heated through. Divide the pasta and oysters equally into six bowls. Garnish with shaved parmesan and bottarga. Enjoy.

Shrimp And Grits Kabobs

Servings:4
Cooking Time: 67 Minutes

Ingredients:
- ¼ cup Pecan oil or butter
- 1 cup country ham finely diced
- ½ cup diced scallions
- ½ cup red pepper finely diced
- ½ cup yellow pepper finely diced
- 1 cup heavy cream
- 4 cups water
- 2 teaspoons salt
- ½ teaspoons black pepper
- ½ teaspoon dried thyme
- 1 cup grits
- 1 cup cheddar cheese, shredded
- 1 pound shrimp, 26-30 count, pealed and deveined, tail on
- ¼ cup olive oil
- 1 Tablespoon Dijon mustard
- 1 teaspoon minced garlic
- 2 Tablespoons fresh lemon juice
- salt and pepper
- 1 red pepper, seeded and membrane removed, cut into 1 inch squares
- 1 yellow pepper, seeded and membrane removed, cut into 1 inch squares
- 1 red onion, peeled, cut in 1 inch squares, separate layers

Directions:
1. Cooked diced ham in butter or oil until almost crisp. Add diced peppers and scallions. Cook until soft. Add cream, water and spices. Bring to a boil, gradually stir in grits. Bring to a boil, them lower to simmer. Continue cooking for 45-60 minutes adding a little more liquid if needed; they need to be thick. Remove from heat and stir in cheese until melted. Pour into greased Rectangular Drip Pan. Chill over night.
2. Combine olive oil, Dijon mustard, garlic, lemon juice, salt and pepper in a bowl. Add shrimp to mixture and marinate about 30 minutes.
3. Cut grits into 1 inch squares. Broil in oven on both sides until golden. Thread Flexible Skewers with 1 grits cube then pierce on one piece each of shrimp, red pepper, yellow pepper, and red onion. Chill until ready to use.
4. Preheat the grill to 350°F using direct heat with a cast iron grate installed. Place skewers on plate setter; close dome and cook 5-7 minutes or until shrimp are opaque.
5. Use spatula to carefully lift from underneath.

Scallops, Asparagus And Artichoke Gratin

Servings:6

Cooking Time: 24 Minutes

Ingredients:

- 1½ lbs U10 sea scallops
- 8 tbsp unsalted butter, divided
- ½ cup finely chopped shallots
- 6 tbsp all-purpose flour
- 2 cups cream
- 1 cup milk
- 1½ cups shaved parmesan cheese, divided
- 2 tsp kosher salt
- ½ tsp ground black pepper
- ½ tsp lemon zest
- ½ tsp crushed red pepper
- 2 pounds asparagus, trimmed and blanched
- 2 (15 ounce) cans artichoke hearts, drained
- 4 tbsp panko bread crumbs
- ½ cup crumbled bacon

Directions:

1. Preheat the grill to 400°F using direct heat with a cast iron grate installed.

2. Melt 4 tablespoons butter in a cast iron skillet; add scallops and cook until almost opaque and slightly browned, turning once. Remove from the skillet.

3. Add the remaining butter and shallots; cook, stirring occasionally about 5 minutes until tender. Stir in flour, cook for one minute. Gradually stir in milk and cream; cook 3 to 4 minutes until thickened. Stir in 1 cup cheese, salt, pepper, lemon zest and red pepper.

4. Add asparagus and artichokes, stirring to coat; cook 10 minutes. Add scallops, top with bread crumbs and bacon; cook 3 to 5 minutes more.

Grilled Lobster

Servings: 4

Cooking Time: 20 Minutes

Ingredients:

- 1/2 bunch of fresh flat-leaf parsley, chopped
- 4 sprigs of fresh thyme, leaves only
- 5 garlic cloves, coarsely chopped
- 1/4 cup unsalted butter, melted
- kosher salt and freshly ground black pepper
- 2 cups panko breadcrumbs
- 2 whole lobsters, about 2lb (1kg) in total, split lengthwise and cleaned at the fish counter
- 2 tbsp olive oil
- lemon wedges, to serve

Directions:

1. Preheat the grill to 400°F (204°C) using direct heat with a cast iron grate installed. In a food processor, combine parsley, thyme, garlic, and butter, and pulse until a cohesive mixture forms. Season with salt and pepper to taste, then add the breadcrumbs and pulse a couple times just to combine.

2. Drizzle lobster with a little oil, then pack the body cavity with the breadcrumb mixture. Place lobsters on the grate shell side down, close the lid, and grill until breadcrumbs are golden brown, about 12 to 18 minutes, keeping the lobster shells between the fire and the tender meat.

3. Remove lobster from the grill, and serve immediately with lemon wedges to squeeze over top.

Foil Packet Fish Filets

Servings: 4

Cooking Time: 15 Minutes

Ingredients:

- 4 (4 oz each) white fish filets
- 1/2 cup white wine
- 4 Tablespoons butter
- 4 pieces heavy duty foil
- 4 sprigs fresh thyme
- 4 green onions, cut in thirds
- 1 zucchini, julienned
- 1 large carrot, julienned
- 1 clove garlic, minced

Directions:

1. On the bottom of each foil sheet, place zucchini, carrot and onion to create a bed.
2. Place one fish filet on each bed of vegetables and top with garlic, thyme, 1 Tbs of butter, salt and pepper to taste.
3. Gather two sides of the foil together and fold down so the foil is almost touching the food.
4. Roll one side of the foil then pour in 2 Tablespoon of white wine. Close the remaining side. Repeat
5. Grilling:
6. Preheat the grill to 375°F using direct heat with a cast iron grate installed.
7. Place the foil packets on the grid and close the dome for 12-15 minutes or until the fish is cooked through.

Cold-smoked Rock Shrimp

Servings:6

Cooking Time: 20 Minutes

Ingredients:

- 2 lb. rock shrimp
- 2 qt. ice
- ½ cup rock salt
- 3 sprigs of parsley
- 3 sprigs of tarragon
- 2 radishes, sliced
- Juice/zest of 6 blood oranges
- 1 cup cider vinegar
- ½ cup sugar
- 1 garlic clove, minced
- ½ tsp Aleppo pepper, or chili of your choice

Directions:

1. Preheat the grill to 250°F using direct heat with a cast iron grate installed.
2. Prep the shrimp by placing them on top of a perforated pan or in aluminum foil with a few holes poked through. Place this pan over an ice/rock salt mixture inside a non-perforated pan.
3. Place ½ of the herbs on the charcoal and ½ on the cooking grid, then add the pan with the shrimp to the kamado grill and cold-smoke for 20 minutes; the shrimp will not be fully cooked.
4. To serve, place some gastrique in the bottom of a bowl, top with shrimp, add some raw radishes and herbs to the top and enjoy!
5. Mix all the gastrique ingredients together and cook until slightly syrupy. Cool, pour over the shrimp, and let marinate for one hour before serving.

Watermelon Pizza

Servings:2

Cooking Time: 12 Minutes

Ingredients:

- 1 Large Watermelon
- 12 Large Shrimp, peeled and deveined
- Sweet & Smoky Seasoning
- 3 TBS olive oil
- 1 cup tomatoes, diced
- 1 Jalapeño, sliced

- 10 sprigs of Cilantro, chopped
- 1 cup of Feta cheese, crumbled
- 4 Bamboo Skewers, soaked
- Salt to taste

Directions:

1. Preheat the grill to 400°F using direct heat with a cast iron grate installed.

2. Skewer the shrimp and season with the olive oil and Sweet & Smoky Seasoning.

3. Cut the Watermelon in a 3-inch diameter. Lightly salt the watermelon.

4. Grill Watermelon 3 minutes on each side and remove from the grill.

5. Grill the shrimp 3 minutes per side and remove from the grill.

6. Build the pizza with the shrimp, feta cheese, jalapeño, tomatoes and cilantro. Grill for another 5 minutes to soften feta and watermelon.

7. Enjoy!

Cajun Shrimp Burgers

Servings:4

Cooking Time: 12 Minutes

Ingredients:

- 1 – 1 1/2 pounds raw shrimp, peeled and deveined
- 4 tablespoons olive oil or coconut oil, divided
- 1 small shallot, finely minced (about 2-3 tablespoons)
- 1 small clove garlic, finely minced
- 1/4 cup red or yellow pepper, finely minced
- 1 teaspoon sea salt
- 1/2 teaspoon freshly ground pepper
- 1 teaspoon chili powder
- 1 teaspoon paprika
- 1 teaspoon cayenne pepper
- 1 teaspoon Dijon mustard
- 1 teaspoon fresh lemon juice
- 1 tablespoon of worcestershire sauce
- 1 large egg, beaten
- 1 green onion, chopped
- 3/4 cup of Coconut Cream (place a can in the refrigerator overnight and scoop the top for the cream and save the rest for your smoothie) or Paleo Mayonnaise
- 1 tablespoon of dijon mustard
- 1 tablespoons of all natural ketchup
- 1 teaspoon of worcestershire sauce
- 1 teaspoon horseradish
- 1 teaspoon of Paprika
- 1 teaspoon fresh lemon juice
- 1/2 teaspoon Cayenne
- 1/2 teaspoon chili powder
- 1/2 teaspoon of Salt

Directions:

1. Preheat the grill to 425°F using direct heat with a cast iron grate installed.

2. Add shrimp to your food processor and pulse until mixture is in small pieces. Remove and place in a mixing bowl.

3. In a small sauté pan, heat 1 tablespoon oil over medium heat. Add shallot, garlic and peppers; cook for about 4 minutes, until softened. Season with salt and pepper. Remove from heat and let cool. Add the remaining ingredients then cooled pepper mixture to the shrimp bowl and combine well. Mold to your desired burger size and set on a plate then cover and refrigerate for 30 minutes.

4. Meanwhile in a small bowl, combine mayonnaise ingredients and set aside.

5. Cook burgers on the Cast Iron Grid for 3-4 minutes per side, until golden brown and cooked through.

Ginger Garlic Shrimp Stir-fry

Servings:6

Cooking Time: 13 Minutes

Ingredients:

- 3 tbsp honey, separated
- 1 tbsp rice wine vinegar
- 1 tbsp soy sauce
- 1 tbsp garlic chili sauce
- 2 tsp freshly grated ginger
- 1 lb. large shrimp, peeled and deveined
- 2 tbsp vegetable oil
- 1 lb. Brussels sprouts, blanched, trimmed, halved
- 1 red bell pepper, diced
- Salt and pepper
- 3 cloves garlic, thinly sliced
- 3 scallions, white and green parts separated and chopped
- 2 tsp toasted sesame oil

Directions:

1. Three hours before cooking, mix together 2 tbsp of honey, vinegar, soy sauce, garlic chili sauce, and ginger in a large bowl. Add shrimp and mix to combine. Cover the bowl and let marinate in the refrigerator.

2. Preheat the grill to 500°F using direct heat with a cast iron grate installed. Add the wok to the kamado grillspander System's platesetter Basket.

3. Heat 1 tablespoon vegetable oil in the wok. Add the Brussels sprouts and the red bell pepper. Sauté for about 5-7 minutes stirring frequently until the Brussels sprouts brown. Pull them out and place in a serving bowl, then drizzle with the remaining honey, salt and pepper; mix together.

4. Add remaining 1 tablespoon vegetable oil to the wok, add garlic and scallion whites then cook for 30 seconds. Remove the shrimp from the marinade and add to the wok. Cook for approximately 4 minutes until the shrimp curl and turn pink.

5. Remove the wok from the kamado grill, and add the shrimp mixture to the serving bowl. Drizzle with sesame oil, top with scallion greens, and toss. Serve immediately.

Roasted Halibut With Greek Relish

Servings:6

Cooking Time: 10 Minutes

Ingredients:

- 2 (14.5 ounce) cans of Red Gold Petite Diced Tomatoes, drained
- 1/4 cup extra virgin olive oil
- 3 cloves garlic, minced
- 1/2 tablespoon kosher salt
- 10 fresh basil leaves, chopped
- 10 ounces Kalamata olives, slices 1/4 inch
- 1 small red onion, diced
- 3 ounces feta cheese, dry
- 2 tablespoons red wine vinegar
- 2 tablespoons canola oil, or salad oil of choice
- 2 pounds fresh halibut filets
- Kosher salt and freshly ground black pepper to taste

Directions:

1. For the relish, blend all ingredients, except the halibut, together and refrigerate for a few hours.

2. Preheat the grill to 400°F using direct heat with a cast iron grate installed.

3. Season halibut filets lightly with salt and black pepper.

4. Place seasoned halibut on kamado grill and roast for 8-10 minutes or until the fish just begins to flake.

5. When fish is almost done, place a small amount of the tomato relish on top of the fish and allow to warm through.

6. Remove fish from heat and place it on a small pile of the tomato relish allowing the heat of the fish to warm the tomato relish through. Serve warm.

Mediterranean Surf And Turf Kabobs

Servings:6
Cooking Time: 20 Minutes

Ingredients:

- 1 lb. boneless leg of lamb (cut into 1 x 1 pieces)
- 1 lb. jumbo shrimp (peeled and deveined)
- 1 red onion (cut into 1 x 1 chunks)
- 1 container baby portobello mushrooms
- 1 container grape tomatoes
- 1 can artichoke hearts
- 1 cup olive oil
- ¼ cup red wine vinegar
- ¼ cup capers (chopped)
- 2 tbsp. fresh oregano (chopped)
- 2 tbsp. fresh rosemary (chopped)
- 2 tbsp. thyme (chopped)
- 1-2 cloves garlic (chopped)
- 1-2 tsp. kosher salt
- ½ tsp. ground black pepper
- ½ tsp. cumin
- ½ tsp. ground coriander

Directions:

1. Preheat the grill to 425°F using direct heat with a cast iron grate installed.

2. You will make 2 different skewers – one will hold the lamb, mushrooms, shrimp and onions. The other will have tomatoes and artichokes. Place the skewers in a pan or dish and pour marinade over them. Toss skewers in marinade and allow marinating for up to 1 hour.

3. Grill the lamb/shrimp skewer for 7-10 minutes or until cooked thoroughly (suggested internal temperature is 135°F). Grill the tomato/artichoke skewer for 3-5 minutes. Take the grilled items off the skewer and serve with either rice or couscous with Tzatziki sauce for a delicious meal!

4. Combine all of the ingredients for the marinade. Set aside.

Bourbon-glazed Cold Smoked Salmon

Servings:8
Cooking Time: 210 Minutes

Ingredients:

- 2-pound salmon filet, skin on
- 1 tablespoon Makers Mark Bourbon
- 1 orange, zested and sliced into rings
- 1 cup kosher salt
- 2 cups dark brown sugar
- 1 cup Makers Mark Bourbon
- 1/3 cup brown sugar
- ½ cup fig jam
- 1 Tbsp orange juice
- 2 tsp Worcestershire sauce
- ¼ tsp dried mustard
- Pinch of garlic

Directions:

1. Lay the salmon skin-side down on a cutting board. Remove any bones from the flesh and

wipe clean of scales. Rinse the salmon with the whiskey and allow to air dry for 10 minutes.

2. In a bowl, combine orange zest, salt and sugar. Line a baking dish with plastic wrap, extending the wrap to allow for wrapping the salmon later. Sprinkle half of the salt mixture on the plastic wrap. Add the salmon and cover with the remaining salt mixture.

3. Lay the orange slices on top of the mixture. Wrap the salmon tightly in the plastic wrap and place in the back of your refrigerator for 48 hours.

4. Once cured, rinse the salmon in cold water. Place the salmon back into the refrigerator, uncovered, for 4 hours.

5. For the glaze, bring bourbon to a boil over medium heat in a saucepan. Add the sugar and whisk, add the remaining ingredients, whisking to blend after each addition. Reduce heat to simmer until sauce is thickened and reduced by half.

6. Preheat the grill to 50°F using direct heat with a cast iron grate installed. Add the salmon to the grid and smoke for 1 hour. Baste the salmon with the bourbon glaze and smoke for an additional 2½ hours.

7. Slice and serve with crackers.

Cedar Planked Honey Glazed Salmon With Grilled Lemon Butter Asparagus

Servings:8
Cooking Time: 20 Minutes

Ingredients:
- 4 7-8 oz salmon fillets, skin on
- Citrus and Herb Seasoning
- Salt and pepper to taste
- 2 Western Cedar Grilling Planks
- ½ cup honey
- 2 tbsp Dijon mustard
- 1 tbsp lemon juice
- ¼ cup Worcestershire sauce
- 1 tsp black pepper
- ½ tsp kosher salt
- 1 tsp cayenne pepper
- 1 bunch asparagus (bottoms trimmed)
- Extra virgin olive oil
- Salt and pepper to taste
- 4 tbsp unsalted butter
- ½ tsp lemon zest
- 2 tbsp lemon juice

Directions:
1. Preheat the grill to 400°F using direct heat with a cast iron grate installed.

2. Soak the planks in water, or ½ water and ½ Chardonnay, using a weight to fully submerge the plank.

3. If cooking a whole side of salmon, cut off the neck end (about 1½ inches) and the tail end (about 3 inches) until the fish is an even thickness. Cut the thin part of the belly off as well. You can use these pieces for salmon dip, or grill separately. We do this to make sure all the filets cook evenly. Cut them to the size you want.

4. Take out the Salmon and place on a plate. Rub with olive oil and season with Citrus & Herb Seasoning.

5. Remove the plank from the water and place on the Egg for 3 minutes to heat.

6. Remove the plank and flip it over (Use BGE Pit Mitts), and place on a tray or cutting board as it will be hot.

7. Take salmon and place on the hot side of the plank.

8. Place on the kamado grill and close the lid. Cook 10-12 minutes.

9. Brush with honey glaze the last 2-3 minutes. Remove and brush one more time with the glaze, Internal temperature of the fish should be 145°F

10. Mix all the ingredients together for the glaze and set aside.

11. Set the kamado grill for direct cooking without a platesetter at 400°F/204°C.

12. Coat the asparagus with extra virgin olive oil and season with salt and pepper. Add the asparagus to the cooking grid and grill until slightly charred and fork tender.

13. Add the butter, lemon zest and lemon juice to the saucepot and place the pot on the cooking grid so that the butter melts while you grill your asparagus.

14. Remove the asparagus from the kamado grill to a platter; pour the butter sauce over the asparagus. Enjoy!

Grilled Fish Tacos

Servings:10
Cooking Time: 5minutes

Ingredients:

- 1 teaspoon cumin
- 1 teaspoon brown sugar
- 1 teaspoon ground coriander
- 2 teaspoons olive oil
- 1½ pounds fresh salmon, halibut, catfish, or your favorite fish
- Corn tortillas
- Lime wedges
- 1½ cups diced fresh peaches
- 1 firm, but ripe avocado, diced
- ¼ cup thinly sliced red onion
- 2 tablespoons chopped fresh cilantro
- ½ small jalapeño, minced
- juice of 1 lime, about 3 tablespoons

Directions:

1. Preheat the grill to 400°F using direct heat with a cast iron grate installed.

2. In a small bowl, combine cumin, sugar, and coriander. Brush fish with olive oil and sprinkle with spice mixture. Grill fish on oiled cooking grid for 3-5 minutes per side until cooked to your liking. Char tortillas on cooking grid, about 10 seconds on each side.

3. Serve tacos with fresh salsa and desired toppings. (cheese, etc.)

4. Combine salsa ingredients in a medium bowl and refrigerate until ready to use.

Grilled Asian Mahi-mahi

Servings:4
Cooking Time: 24 Minutes

Ingredients:

- 4 (1 inch thick) Mahi-Mahi filets
- 1 tablespoon Better Than Bouillon Fish Base
- ½ cup soy sauce
- 1 ½ Tablespoon sesame oil
- 1 teaspoon honey
- ½ teaspoon garlic powder
- 2 teaspoons sesame seeds

Directions:

1. Preheat the grill to 400°F using direct heat with a cast iron grate installed.

2. Mix the fish base, soy sauce, sesame oil, honey and garlic powder in a medium-sized shallow bowl. Add the Mahi-Mahi to the bowl and marinate for 20 minutes.

3. Place the Mahi-Mahi directly onto the kamado grill and grill for 3-4 minutes per side.

4. Remove the fish from the grill, sprinkle with the sesame seeds and serve immediately.

Cigar Dave's Alpha-meal

Servings:4
Cooking Time: 20minutes

Ingredients:

- Salmon
- Plank
- Cajun Seasoning
- Lemon

Directions:

1. Preheat the grill to 375°F using direct heat with a cast iron grate installed.
2. Place salmon on plank and flavor with Cajun seasoning and lemon.
3. Cook on kamado grill for 20 minutes. Serve with a glass of bourbon!

Grilled Shrimp, Romaine And Avocado Salad

Servings:6
Cooking Time: 10 Minutes

Ingredients:

- 18 medium shrimp, peeled and deveined
- 3 hearts of romaine lettuce
- 3 firm avocados
- 3 tbsp (45 ml) olive oil
- Salt and pepper
- 24 cherry tomatoes, cut in half
- 8 oz (225 g) natural goat cheese
- 1 cup (240 ml) skinless unsalted peanuts, cut into fine pieces
- 1/3 cup (80 ml) lemon juice
- 2 tbsp (30 ml) water
- 2 tbsp (30 ml) chopped parsley
- Salt and pepper
- 2/3 cup (160 ml) extra virgin olive oil

Directions:

1. Divide the goat cheese into 12 balls and coat the cheese balls by rolling them over the peanuts. Set aside. Place the cut tomatoes in a bowl and season with salt and pepper. Set aside.
2. Preheat the grill to 400°F using direct heat with a cast iron grate installed.
3. Skewer the shrimp and brush with olive oil. Add to the grid and grill three to four minutes, turning once, until they are opaque. Cut the avocados lengthways in halves without removing the peel; remove the pit. Brush each half with olive oil. Season with salt and pepper, and place peel side up on the grill for three to four minutes until they have nice grid marks.
4. Cut the romaine hearts lengthways in halves. Brush each half with olive oil. Season with salt and pepper, and place cut side down on the grill for one minute. Assemble with the shrimp, tomatoes, avocados and cheese balls and drizzle with vinaigrette. Serve immediately.
5. Shake all vinaigrette ingredients in a bottle until emulsified. Reserve.

Cioppino (chip-ee-no)

Servings: 6
Cooking Time: 50 Minutes

Ingredients:

- 1 1/2 lbs halibut, or other firm fish, cut into 2 inch chunks
- 1 lb clams, scrubbed
- 1 lb mussels, scrubbed and debearded
- 1 lb shrimp, peeled and deveined
- 4 cloves garlic, minced
- 1 large fennel bulb, thinly sliced
- 1 onion, thinly sliced
- 5 cups chicken or fish stock
- 1 1/2 cups dry white wine
- 1/4 cup tomato paste

- 3 Tablespoons olive oil
- 1 tsp crushed red chile flakes
- 1 (28 ounce) can diced tomatoes

Directions:

1. Preheat the grill to 350°F using direct heat with a cast iron grate installed with the dutch oven on the grid.

2. Heat the oil in the dutch oven and add fennel, onion, and garlic and cook until translucent.

3. Stir in tomato paste and chili flake and cook for 1 minute.

4. Add diced tomatoes with their juice, wine, and stock and cover with the lid.

5. Lower the dome for 30 minutes.

6. Remove the lid of the dutch oven and add the clams and mussels.

7. Replace the lid and lower the dome for 5 minutes.

8. Remove the lid of the dutch oven and add the shrimp and fish and gently stir.

9. Replace the lid and lower the dome for 5 minutes.

10. When the fish is cooked through, the shrimp are pink, and the mussels and clams are open, the stew is done.

11. Serve immediately with crusty sourdough bread.

Crab Quiche

Servings:8
Cooking Time: 30 Minutes

Ingredients:

- 3⁄4 cup diced crabmeat or diced faux crab
- 1 medium red bell pepper, diced (about 3⁄4cup) 1⁄2 cup shredded sharp cheddar cheese
- 3 large eggs
- 3⁄4 cup milk
- 1⁄2 teaspoon salt
- 1⁄4 teaspoon black pepper
- 2 whole, trimmed scallions, chopped
- 3⁄4 cup King Arthur Unbleached All-Purpose Flour
- 1⁄4 cup Hi-maize Fiber; or substitute 1/4 cup all-purpose flour*
- 1⁄4 cup Vermont cheese powder
- 1⁄4 teaspoon salt
- 1⁄4 teaspoon paprika, hot, sweet, or smoked
- Pinch of cayenne pepper, optional
- 6 tablespoons cold unsalted butter, diced
- 1⁄4 cup shredded sharp cheddar cheese
- 2 tablespoons (1 ounce) ice water*
- *If you substitute flour for the Hi-maize, increase the water by 1 tablespoon.

Directions:

1. Combine the crabmeat, died pepper and cheese; set aside. Whisk together the eggs, milk, salt and pepper.

2. Preheat the grill to 400°F using direct heat with a cast iron grate installed.

3. Roll the dough on a BGE Dough Rolling Mat into a 12 inch circle and place it into the Deep Dish Pizza/Baking Stone. Add the crab mixture, then pour in the milk-egg mixture. Sprinkle with the chopped scallions.

4. Bake the quiche for 27 to 30 minutes, until it's barely set in the center. Remove from the kamado grill and let it cool for 10 minutes before serving.

5. Whisk together the flour, Hi-maize, cheese powder, salt, paprika and cayenne. Work the butter into the flour to form coarse crumbs. Toss in the cheese.

6. Drizzle in the water, stirring until the dough is cohesive; add more water if necessary. Pat the dough into a disk, wrap, and refrigerate for 30 minutes.

POULTRY

Lemon Pepper Wings

Servings:4

Cooking Time: 16 Minutes

Ingredients:

- Feta Dipping Sauce
- ½ cup mayonnaise
- ½ cup sour cream
- ½ cup feta cheese
- 2 teaspoons red wine vinegar
- 1 teaspoon Worcestershire sauce
- Kosher salt and freshly ground black pepper
- ¼ cup lemon zest, lemons reserved (about 6 medium lemons)
- ½ cup extra-virgin olive oil
- 2 tablespoons granulated garlic
- 1 tablespoon kosher salt
- 1 tablespoon freshly ground black pepper
- 2 pounds chicken wings

Directions:

1. Preheat the grill to 500°F using direct heat with a cast iron grate installed.

2. Mix the mayonnaise, sour cream, cheese, vinegar, and Worcestershire sauce in a small bowl. Season with salt and pepper, blend well, and refrigerate.

3. Mix the lemon zest and olive oil in a small bowl and set aside. Mix the garlic, salt, and pepper in a medium bowl. Reserve 1 tablespoon of the garlic seasoning for later use.

4. Toss the chicken with the remaining 3 tablespoons of seasoning.

5. Place the chicken on the cooking grid and baste with the olive oil mixture. Close the lid of the kamado grill. Turn the chicken wings every few minutes, basting often, closing the lid each time. Grill for 15 minutes, or until golden brown and slightly crisp. Season with the reserved garlic mixture and cook for another minute.

6. Transfer the chicken wings to a platter, squeeze the reserved lemons over the wings, and serve immediately with the dressing.

Smoked Chicken Wings

Servings:8

Cooking Time: 120 Minutes

Ingredients:

- 3 dozen chicken wings
- Sweet & Smoky or Savory Pecan Seasoning
- Habanero Hot Sauce

Directions:

1. Preheat the grill to 225°F using direct heat with a cast iron grate installed.

2. Rub 3 dozen wings liberally with Sweet & Smoky or Savory Pecan Seasoning. Smoke the wings, turning occasionally, for 1 1/2 to 2 hours or until the internal temperature reaches 165°F or higher.

3. Toss the wings in the Habanero hot sauce.

Garfunkel Chicken

Servings:6

Cooking Time: 50 Minutes

Ingredients:

- 1 whole young chicken, 3 to 4 pounds
- 1/2 cup olive oil
- 1 tbsp parsley
- 1 tbsp rubbed sage
- 1 tbsp rosemary
- 1 tsp ground thyme
- 1/2 tsp salt

- 1/2 tsp black pepper

Directions:

1.   Remove the backbone from the chicken with either poultry shears or a sharp knife. Turn the chicken over and press down to flatten and break the cartilage in the breast. Rub the entire bird with the olive oil. Mix the herbs and spices together and sprinkle these over the entire bird.

2.   Preheat the grill to 350°F using direct heat with a cast iron grate installed. Cook the chicken skin side down for about 15 to 20 minutes until the skin is browned and crispy.

3.   Flip the chicken over to bone side down and cook for another 25 to 30 minutes until the internal temperature in the breast is 160°F.

Grilled Duck Breast With Apple Brandy Glaze

Servings:10

Cooking Time: 40 Minutes

Ingredients:

- 4 duck breasts
- 2 tbsp (30 ml) salt
- 2 tbsp (30 ml) black pepper
- 2 tbsp (30 ml) paprika
- 2 chorizo sausage links, meat removed from the casing
- 2 tbsp (30 ml) parsley, chopped
- 3 sage leaves, chopped
- 1½ cups (360 ml) dried cornbread (fresh or bagged)
- ¾ cup (180 ml) chicken stock
- 1½ tbsp (22 ml) extra virgin olive oil
- 1 whole diced shallot or ¼ cup (60 ml) small diced yellow sweet onion
- Salt and pepper, to taste
- ½ cup (120 ml) apple brandy
- 1 cup (240 ml) apple juice
- 2 tbsp (30 ml) sugar
- 1 cup (240 ml) fresh or frozen cranberries
- 1 cup (240 ml) triple sec
- 4 tbsp (60 ml) sugar
- Zest and juice of one medium orange

Directions:

1.   Preheat the grill to 375°F using direct heat with a cast iron grate installed.

2.   Using a small knife cut a small pocket in each duck breasts, making sure that the pocket goes all the way through the middle of the breast to the other end; do not butterfly the breast. Gently stuff 2 to 4 tbsp (30 to 60 ml) of the chorizo stuffing into each duck breast.

3.   Season both sides of the duck with salt, black pepper and paprika. Grill stuffed duck breast, fat side down first, for 8 to 10 minutes on each side until golden brown.

4.   Liberally brush glaze on each side of the duck with Apple Brandy Glaze. Let rest on the cutting board for 5 to 7 minutes before cutting; this will allow the juices to distribute evenly and give the duck a resting temperature of 140-145°F for medium doneness. Slice duck breast into ¾ in/2 cm medallions. Serve immediately.

5.   Preheat the grill to 350°F using direct heat with a cast iron grate installed.

6.   Add olive oil to a Stir-fry & Paella Pan, add chorizo and stir occasionally until cooked through. Add shallot, brown until golden. Add chicken stock and bring to a boil.

7.   Remove the Pan from the kamado grill, fold in cornbread, chopped parsley and chopped sage until well incorporated, and cornbread stuffing is moist. Season to taste with salt and pepper. Allow cornbread-sage stuffing to cool before stuffing duck breasts.

8. Pour all ingredients into a Stir-fry & Paella Pan, whisk together and bring to a boil. Reduce heat to 300°F; simmer until sauce forms a glaze consistency, about 20 minutes. Remove glaze from the kamado grill, allow glaze to cool.

9. In a Stir-fry & Paella Pan, combine triple sec, sugar, orange juice and zest; bring to a boil. Add cranberries and cook until cranberries start to pop. Reduce heat to 300°F, until cranberry-orange sauce turns to sauce/glaze consistency; check for desired sauce sweetness at this point.

Champagne Quail

Servings:6
Cooking Time: 25 Minutes

Ingredients:

- 12 quail (or chicken breast)
- 2 Tablespoons poultry seasoning
- 12 strips of bacon
- ¾ cup melted butter
- 2 cups champagne

Directions:

1. Preheat the grill to 350°F using direct heat with a cast iron grate installed.

2. Clean the quail and pat dry. Season with poultry seasoning. Wrap bacon around quail; secure with toothpicks. Melt butter in a Drip Pan; add quail and champagne to the pan. Cover pan securely with aluminum foil, place on cooking grid and cook for 20-25 minutes or desired internal temperature is reached.

Smoked Wings With Moonshine White Sauce And Ranch Pickles

Servings:12
Cooking Time: 136 Minutes

Ingredients:

- 3 dozen Springer Mountain Farms Chicken Wings

Directions:

1. Preheat the grill to 225°F using direct heat with a cast iron grate installed. Rub 3 dozen wings liberally with BBQ Rub seasoning. Smoke for 1½ to 2 hours or until the internal temperature reaches 165°F or higher.

2. Remove wings from heat and toss with half of the Moonshine White Sauce set aside and bring the kamado grill up to 425°F. Put wings back on the kamado grill for 8 minutes then flip and cook for another 8 minutes on other side. Toss with remaining Moonshine White Sauce. Serve immediately with Ranch Pickles.

Bacon-wrapped Bbq Quail

Servings:12
Cooking Time: 24 Minutes

Ingredients:

- 12 bone in quail halves
- 3 tablespoons Savory Pecan Seasoning
- 1 lb bacon
- 1 cup Vidalia Onion and Sriracha Barbecue Sauce

Directions:

1. Preheat the grill to 350°F using direct heat with a cast iron grate installed.

2. Season each quail half with Savory Pecan Seasoning; wrap each half in a slice of bacon and secure with a toothpick.

3. Grill the quail for 8 to 10 minutes per side or until the bacon is cooked through. When the quail is almost finished, brush with the sauce. Flip the quail and baste the other side. Grill for an additional 3 to 4 minutes to caramelize the glaze.

Lemon Scented Chicken Thighs

Servings: 8

Cooking Time: 40 Minutes

Ingredients:

- 2-3 lbs bone in, skin on chicken thighs
- 1 recipe Lemon Rosemary Marinade
- 1 lemon, thinly sliced

Directions:

1. In a large zip top bag, pour marinade over chicken thighs and refrigerate for 30 minutes.
2. Grilling:
3. Preheat the grill to 375°F using direct heat with a cast iron grate installed.
4. Remove the thighs from the marinade and gently slide thinly sliced lemon between the skin and the meat.
5. Place thighs directly on the grid, skin side down, and close the dome for 20 minutes.
6. Turn the thighs and close the dome for an additional 15-20 minutes or until the internal temperature reaches 170°F.

O'neill Williams' Turkey Parmesan

Servings:4

Cooking Time: 35 Minutes

Ingredients:

- 2 egg whites
- 1 Tbsp water
- ½ cup Italian-seasoned dry bread crumbs
- 2 Tbsp freshly grated Parmesan cheese
- 1 lb. boneless turkey breast fillets (chicken can be used)
- 1 cup Italian-flavored tomato sauce
- 1 cup shredded mozzarella cheese

Directions:

1. Preheat the grill to 400°F using direct heat with a cast iron grate installed.
2. In a shallow bowl, beat egg whites with water. In another shallow bowl, combine bread crumbs and Parmesan cheese. Dip turkey into egg whites and then dredge in bread crumb mixture; place in a 13 X 9 pan.
3. Place pan on the cooking grid and bake 30 minutes. Pour tomato sauce evenly over the turkey and top with mozzarella cheese.
4. Bake 5 more minutes or until turkey is cooked through.

Cuban Chicken Bombs

Servings:4

Cooking Time: 30 Minutes

Ingredients:

- 4 bone in chicken thighs
- 4 slices of ham (cut into quarters)
- 4 slices of provolone (cut into quarters)
- 2 tbsp Dijon mustard
- 12 pickle chips
- 8 slices of bacon
- Sweet & Smoky Seasoning

Directions:

1. Preheat the grill to 300°F using direct heat with a cast iron grate installed.
2. Debone the chicken thighs leaving the skin on and position the chicken thighs skin side down. Spread equal portions of the mustard on the meat side of each chicken thigh. Place an equal amount of provolone slices, ham and pickles on each chicken thigh. Roll the chicken thighs up and wrap a piece of bacon around the middle of the chicken thigh and another around the thigh lengthwise sealing the contents with bacon. Put toothpicks through the bottom of the chicken thighs to help keep contents inside while

cooking. Season the top of the bacon with the Sweet & Smokey Seasoning.

3. Cook the chicken for about an hour or until the internal temperature reaches 165°F. Remove the chicken from the kamado grill and let rest before slicing and serving.

Hatch Chile Salsa And Chicken Casserole

Servings:6
Cooking Time: 55 Minutes

Ingredients:

- 5 boneless, skinless chicken breasts
- 32 oz. shredded cheddar cheese
- 32 oz. chicken stock
- 5-6 large tortillas
- ¼ cup Cotija cheese
- 15-20 Hatch chiles
- 1 small onion or ½ large onion
- 4 cloves garlic
- 1 bunch cilantro
- 1 tsp cumin
- ½ tsp coriander
- 2 limes, juiced
- 2 tsp honey
- Salt to taste

Directions:

1. Preheat the grill to 400°F using direct heat with a cast iron grate installed.

2. In the dutch oven, cover the chicken with chicken broth and 2 tbsp of the hatch chile salsa. Place on the grill and simmer until the internal temperature reaches 165°F, about 15 minutes. Remove from the grill, strain and chop the chicken.

3. In the same dutch oven, spread a tablespoon of salsa on the bottom. Next place a tortilla and top with chicken and a handful of cheese. Repeat this process until the ingredients are gone. Place on the grill and bake for 20 minutes or until the cheese is melted. During the last 5 minutes top with the Cotija cheese. Remove from the kamado grill and let rest for 10-15 minutes. Enjoy!

4. Preheat the grill to 400°F using direct heat with a cast iron grate installed.

5. Roast the Hatch chiles for 5 minutes per side or until there is a charred outside. Remove the chiles from the grill and place in a gallon-sized resealable bag for 10-15 minutes. The chiles should be soft and pliable at this point. Remove the skins, stems and seeds from the chiles.

6. To give the salsa even more of a roasted flavor you can also roast the onion, garlic and lime, however, this is an optional step. Put all the ingredients for the salsa in a blender or a food processor and blend together to desired consistency. Set aside.

Barbecue Chicken With Alabama White Sauce

Servings:4
Cooking Time: 40 Minutes

Ingredients:

- 4 egg yolks
- ¼ cup apple cider vinegar
- ¼ cup water
- 2 tablespoons poultry seasoning
- 2 tablespoons salt
- 1 cup grapeseed oil
- 6 chicken leg/thigh pieces
- approx. 1 ½ cups Alabama white barbecue sauce
- 2 egg yolks
- ¼ cup lemon juice
- 3 tablespoons apple cider vinegar

- 2 teaspoons salt
- ½ teaspoon garlic powder
- ½ teaspoon cayenne pepper
- 2 teaspoons ground black pepper
- 1 cup grapeseed oil

Directions:

1. In a food processor fitted with a metal blade, blend the egg yolks, vinegar, water, poultry seasoning, and salt until the yolks fluff a little, about 30 seconds. With the processor running, slowly drizzle in the oil, the mixture will blend, emulsify, and resemble a thick mayonnaise. You will hear the sound change to a whop, whop; it should take about 1 minute. Spoon the marinade into a large zip-top bag, add the chicken pieces, and massage until the chicken is completely covered with the marinade. Zip the top closed, pressing out any air as you seal the bag. Set the bag in a bowl in the refrigerator overnight or for up to 24 hours.

2. Pour ¾ cup of the Alabama white barbecue sauce into a bowl to use for basting. Preheat the grill to 400°F using direct heat with a cast iron grate installed. Remove the chicken from the marinade and pat completely dry. Scrape the cooking grid clean and coat with oil. Place the chicken, skin side down, on the grid and cover with an aluminum drip pan or tent with foil. After 10 minutes, flip the chicken pieces. Cover again with the pan or foil. After 10 more minutes, baste the chicken with the sauce, flip so the skin side is down, and baste again. Cover with the pan or foil, cook for another 10 minutes, and then baste, flip, and cover again. Cook, baste, flip, and cover one last time, for a total cooking time of 40 minutes. Discard the basting sauce. Remove the chicken from the grill and rest, tented with foil

or a foil pan, for 10 minutes. Serve with remaining sauce on the side.

3. In a food processor fitted with a metal blade, combine the egg yolks, lemon juice, vinegar, salt, garlic powder, cayenne, and black pepper and process until the yolks fluff a little, about 30 seconds. With the processor running, slowly drizzle in the oil; the mixture will blend and emulsify but won't be as thick as the marinade used for the barbecue chicken. You will again hear the sound change to a whop, whop; it should take about a minute.

Vidalia Onion And Sriracha-glazed Nashville Hot Wings

Servings:4
Cooking Time: 35 Minutes

Ingredients:
- 1 pound whole chicken wings
- 1 tbsp olive oil
- Nashville Hot Seasoning, to taste
- ½ bottle of Vidalia Onion and Sriracha Sauce

Directions:

1. Preheat the grill to 350°F using direct heat with a cast iron grate installed.

2. Separate the flats from the drumettes, discarding the wing tips. Coat with the olive oil and a generous amount of the Nashville Hot Seasoning.

3. Place the wings skin-side down on the grid and cook for 15 minutes. Flip the wings after 15 minutes and cook for another 15-20 minutes, or until the wings measure 175°F internally. Remove the wings and place in a bowl.

4. Pour in ½ bottle of the Vidalia Onion and Sriracha Sauce and stir to coat the wings while they are still hot. Serve and enjoy!

Rosemary Grilled Chicken Sandwiches

Servings:4
Cooking Time: 8 Minutes

Ingredients:

- 4 (4-ounce) boneless, skinless chicken breast halves, fat trimmed
- 3 tablespoons olive oil
- 2 tablespoons fresh lemon juice
- 1 tablespoon finely chopped fresh rosemary
- 2 teaspoons minced garlic (2 medium cloves)
- ½ teaspoon salt
- ¼ teaspoon freshly ground black pepper
- 8 slices Cabot Sharp Cheddar
- 4 ounces sliced Black Forest or other flavorful ham
- 4 buns, split
- Romaine leaves

Directions:

1. Place chicken between 2 large sheets plastic wrap; pound with mallet or heavy pan to flatten to even ½-inch thickness.
2. In medium bowl, whisk together oil, lemon juice, rosemary, garlic, salt and pepper; add chicken, turning to coat. Cover and refrigerate for about 1 hour.
3. Preheat the grill to 500°F using direct heat with a cast iron grate installed.
4. Remove chicken from marinade, shaking off excess. Cook on kamado grill until browned on outside and cooked through to center, 2 to 3 minutes per side. Toward end of cooking time, top each breast with slice of ham and cheese; cover with grill lid or foil until cheese is melted, about 2 minutes longer.
5. Serve on buns with bed of romaine leaves (toast buns on grill if desired).

Polynesian Duck Kabobs

Servings:8
Cooking Time: 15 Minutes

Ingredients:

- 6- 7.5 oz Maple Leaf Farms Boneless Duck Breast Filets, thawed if frozen
- Salt and fresh ground black pepper, to taste
- 1 ripe fresh pineapple, peeled and cored
- 2 large red or yellow bell peppers, or one of each
- 2 large green bell peppers
- 2 small red onions
- 2⁄3 cup pineapple preserves
- 3 tablespoons dijon mustard

Directions:

1. Preheat the grill to 350°F using direct heat with a cast iron grate installed.
2. Remove skin from duck breasts. Cut duck breast into 2 inch chunks; season with salt and pepper to taste.
3. Cut pineapple into 1½ inch chunks. Cut bell peppers into 1½ inch chunks, discarding stems and seeds. Cut onions through the core into ½ inch thick wedges. Alternately thread duck, pineapple, bell peppers and onions onto Flexible Skewers.
4. Combine preserves and mustard; mix well. Arrange duck kabobs on kamado grill. Brush half of preserve mixture over kabobs. Grill covered 5 minutes. Turn; brush remaining half of preserve mixture over kabobs. Continue grilling covered 5 to 6 minutes or until duck is barely pink in center and peppers are crisp-tender.

Open-faced Leftover Turkey Sandwich

Servings:4
Cooking Time: 14 Minutes

Ingredients:

- Sourdough bread
- 3 tsp butter, separated
- Mashed potatoes
- Stuffing or dressing
- Gravy
- Roasted turkey
- Cranberry chutney or cranberry sauce
- Salt and pepper to taste
- Arugula, optional

Directions:

1. Preheat the grill to 400°F using direct heat with a cast iron grate installed.

2. Melt one tablespoon of butter in the cast iron skillet or plancha and add the mashed potatoes. Once they have a nice crust remove and set aside. Next, add the stuffing with gravy and a tablespoon of butter. Once warmed, about 5-7 minutes, remove and set aside. Lastly, add the turkey with more gravy. Once warmed, about 5-7 minutes, remove and set aside.

3. Toast the bread with a tablespoon of butter and salt and pepper. Then pile on the cranberry chutney or sauce! Next, comes the turkey. Follow it up with the mash potatoes and stuffing. Then drizzle more gravy over. Top with arugula and serve immediately.

Smoky Thai Pulled Chicken Sandwiches

Servings:12
Cooking Time: 90 Minutes

Ingredients:

- 3 lbs boneless skinless chicken thighs
- 1 package of Cobblestone Bread Co.™ Sesame Twist Hamburger Rolls
- 3 tbs chopped cilantro
- quick pickled carrots
- * optional Sriracha sauce
- 3 cups water
- 2 tbs pure cane sugar
- juice of one lime
- 2 tsp Thai fish sauce
- 2 tsp soy sauce
- 1 tbs sea salt
- 1-2 hot peppers (Thai bird or Serrano)
- 2 cloves of garlic
- 1 tbs pure cane sugar
- 2 tsp sea salt
- 1 tsp onion powder
- ½ tsp ground ginger
- ½ tsp garlic powder
- ¼ tsp ground white pepper
- ¼ cup water
- ¼ cup honey
- 1 tbs fresh lime juice
- 2 tbs soy sauce
- 1 tsp Thai fish sauce (add while mixing, do not heat)
- ⅔ pound carrots
- 2½ cups water
- ⅔ cup rice wine vinegar
- 1 tbs pure cane sugar
- 2 tsp sea salt
- 2 tsp fresh grated ginger

Directions:

1. Whisk together ingredients for the brine. Add the chicken thighs, making sure they are fully covered. Place in refrigerator for 2-3 hours.

2. Preheat the grill to 280°F using direct heat with a cast iron grate installed.

3. Whisk together the dry rub ingredients. Remove the chicken thighs from brine, and pat dry. Discard brine. Generously coat the chicken with dry rub.

4. Place chicken thighs on the kamado grill. Cook for 1½ hours, flipping once after about 50 minutes. Check temperature occasionally to make sure you are not gout over a maximum of 325°F, damper more narrowly to reduce temperature closer to 280°F.

5. Prepare the Quick Pickled Carrots while the chicken is grilling.

6. When chicken thighs are removed from the kamado grill, set aside to rest and cool a little, then pull the chicken (discard any fatty bits). Mix in chopped fresh cilantro.

7. Mix sauce ingredients, except fish sauce, in a small saucepan over medium-high heat. Once it comes to a boil, reduce to a simmer. Allow to gently bubble for 2 minutes, then shut off and pour over the pulled chicken. Mix. Add fish sauce and mix again.

8. Place some of the pickled matchstick carrots on the bottom half of each Cobblestone Bread Co.™ Sesame Twist Hamburger Roll. Top with a generous helping of the Thai pulled chicken (squirt on a bit of sriracha sauce if you like) and cover with top of the roll.

9. Peel and trim carrots, then matchstick slice.

10. Whisk together pickling brine ingredients in a deep microwave-safe bowl. Microwave for 2 minutes, then whisk again to ensure salt & sugar are dissolved. Add the carrots. Make sure they are fully covered in the brine.

11. Microwave until the brine come to a quick boil (about 5-6 minutes). Microwave for another minute (you may need to stop it a couple times to avoid boil over). Remove from the microwave and set aside to cool.

12. When the brine has cooled to room temperature, drain. Refrigerate the carrots until ready to go on sandwiches.

Hop's Hawaiian Bbq Chicken Pizza

Servings:4
Cooking Time: 17 Minutes

Ingredients:
- 1 lb pizza dough
- 4 oz chopped chicken
- 2 oz chopped ham
- 4 oz chopped pineapple
- Your favorite BBQ sauce
- 1/4 cup shredded cheddar
- 1/2 cup shredded mozzarella

Directions:
1. Preheat the grill to 550°F using direct heat with a cast iron grate installed.

2. I soaked my chicken breast in pineapple juice and BBQ sauce for an hour before I threw it on the kamado grill. Once it was done, I chopped off what I needed for the pie and ate the rest.

3. Next, I added the Pizza Stone, heat the stone before putting your pizza in the kamado grill. If you're good at making your own pizza dough, then you're ahead of me already. I got mine from the grocery store and rolled it out over a bed of finely ground corn meal so it doesn't stick to the counter; I prefer cornmeal to flour.

4. Throw some corn meal on the hot stone in the kamado grill and place the dough on it, close the lid and cook the dough for about 2 minutes per side. This will make a crispier crust and will

make it easier to handle with the ingredients on it.

5. Remove the dough from the kamado grill and spread on the BBQ sauce. Now you're ready for the ham, chicken, pineapple and cheese. If you want more chicken, add more chicken. If you want more cheese, add more cheese. It's pizza, for crying out loud! Put the pie back into the kamado grill and cook it covered for 12-15 minutes or until properly browned.

Brined Roasted Turkey

Servings:4
Cooking Time: 240 Minutes

Ingredients:
- 4 qts water
- 1 ½ cup kosher salt
- ½ cup sugar
- 2 bay leaves
- 2 tbsp black peppercorns
- 1 tbsp dried sage
- 1 orange, cut in half
- 1 lemon, cut in half
- 1 onion, cut in half
- 8 cloves of garlic
- Enough ice to fill the bottom of the brining bucket about 3 inches
- 1 12-14 lb. whole turkey
- 1 orange, cut into wedges
- 1 sweet onion, cut into wedges
- 1 lemon, cut into wedges
- 2 whole heads of garlic, top cut off
- 3 sprigs rosemary
- 3 sprigs thyme
- 3 sprigs sage
- Savory Pecan Seasoning
- Extra virgin olive oil or canola oil
- Kosher salt

Directions:
1. A day before your cook, put all the brine ingredients, except for ice, into a pot and boil for 10 minutes. Pour liquid over ice into the brining bucket. Once the liquid is cool place the turkey into the bucket, making sure the turkey is completely submerged. Cover tightly, and put into the fridge and brine for 8-24 hours. When ready to cook, remove the turkey from the brine and rinse thoroughly.

2. Preheat the grill to 350°F using direct heat with a cast iron grate installed.

3. Pat the turkey dry and coat with oil, season with salt and Savory Pecan Seasoning.

4. Place half of the onion, one whole head of garlic, half the orange, half the lemon, and two sprigs of each herb inside the cavity of the turkey. Fold the wings back behind the turkey so that they cook evenly. Put the turkey on the roasting rack and place into the drip pan. Add the remaining garlic, onion, orange, lemon and herbs around the turkey in the drip pan.

5. Place on the kamado grill and cook 3-4 hours or until the internal temperature is 165°F (white meat) and 185°F (dark meat). During the cook, cover the turkey with aluminum foil once the skin has the desired color and texture.

6. Remove from the kamado grill, let rest for 15 minutes. Carve and enjoy!

Whole Smoked Barbecue Chicken

Servings: 4
Cooking Time: 180 Minutes

Ingredients:
- 2 (2-3 lb) whole chickens
- 1 recipe Basic Barbecue Rub

- 2 cups apple wood chips, soaked for 30 minutes in water

Directions:

1. Generously sprinkle chickens with Basic Barbecue Rub inside and out and set aside.
2. Grilling:
3. Preheat the grill to 225°F using direct heat with a cast iron grate installed.
4. Add wood chips to the charcoal and replace the grid.
5. Place the chickens directly on the grid and close the dome.
6. Cook at 225°F for 3 - 3 1/2 hours or until the internal temperature of the thigh reaches 170°F.
7. Remove the chickens from the grill and allow them to rest for 10 minutes before carving.
8. Serve with your favorite barbecue sauce.

Smoky Grilled Chicken Nachos

Servings:8
Cooking Time: 18 Minutes

Ingredients:

- 5 Mesquite Grilled Chicken Breasts
- 2 cups cheese, shredded
- 1 cup corn
- 1 cup pinto beans
- 1 teaspoon black pepper
- 1 teaspoon creole seasoning
- 1 teaspoon garlic powder
- 1 teaspoon onion powder
- ½ teaspoon oregano, crushed
- 1 tablespoon extra virgin olive oil
- blue corn chips
- yellow corn chips
- jalapenos, sliced
- tomatoes, diced
- avocado, diced
- green onions, sliced

- sour cream

Directions:

1. Mix seasoning blend and set aside.
2. Preheat the grill to 350°F using direct heat with a cast iron grate installed.
3. Place marinated chicken in a bowl, drizzle with olive oil.
4. Sprinkle half the seasoning blend on chicken and mix well.
5. Place chicken on the cooking grid and cook 4-5 minutes per side. Remove chicken from kamado grill and rest before slicing. While chicken is grilling, rinse, drain, corn and beans.
6. Place ½ tablespoon of olive oil into a skillet over medium heat, add corn and beans, season with remaining seasoning blend, sauté for about 5 minutes.
7. Place chips on a round pizza pan, top with bean and corn mixture, cheese, and chicken. Place on the cooking grid and cook for 2-3 minutes, until cheese melts. Top with remaining ingredients.

Lamb Shawarma

Servings:6
Cooking Time: 65 Minutes

Ingredients:

- ¼ cup extra-virgin olive oil
- 3 garlic cloves, minced
- 1 lemon, juiced
- ½ tbsp ground cumin
- ½ tbsp ground cardamom
- ½ tsp Aleppo pepper or ½ teaspoon crushed red pepper
- Freshly ground black pepper
- Kosher salt
- One 2-3 pound butterflied leg of lamb
- 1 medium red onion, cut in half

* 3-4 bamboo skewers
* Yogurt-Tahini Sauce
* Pita bread

Directions:

1. Mix the olive oil with the garlic, lemon juice, cumin, cardamom, red pepper, ½ teaspoon of black pepper and 1 tablespoons of salt. Rub the marinade on the lamb. Refrigerate for 3 days.

2. Preheat the grill to 400°F using direct heat with a cast iron grate installed.

3. Using 3-4 Bamboo skewers, skewer the lamb to one large tower. Use the onion halves on the top and bottom so it will stand on a roasting pan.

4. Roast the lamb until an instant-read thermometer inserted into the thickest part of the meat registers 145°, about 1 hour. Transfer the lamb to a carving board and let rest for 10 minutes.

5. Coat the pita bread with olive oil and toast for about 5 minutes.

6. Thinly slice the lamb across the grain and serve with the Yogurt-Tahini Sauce and Pita Bread.

Savory Beer Can Chicken

Servings:4
Cooking Time: 30 Minutes

Ingredients:

* 1 (4 to 5-pound) chicken
* 1 (12-ounce) can beer
* ¼ cup (60 ml) mayonnaise
* 3 Tbsp (45 ml) Savory Pecan Seasoning

Directions:

1. Preheat the grill to 350°F using direct heat with a cast iron grate installed.

2. Pour ½ of the beer into a drip pan. Place the can with the remaining beer in the center of the Folding Beer Can Chicken Roaster and snap the arms into place at the top.

3. Put the rack into the drip pan and place the chicken onto the rack. Combine the mayonnaise and the seasoning and coat the outer skin and inner cavity of the chicken with the mixture.

4. Roast the chicken until the internal temperature reaches 165ºF/74ºC; remove from the kamado grill and let rest for 10 minutes. Carve and serve.

Grilled Chicken Fajita Skewers

Servings:8
Cooking Time: 8 Minutes

Ingredients:

* ½ cup finely chopped cilantro leaves
* ⅓ cup lime juice (about 6 limes)
* ⅓ cup extra-virgin olive oil
* 4 garlic cloves, minced
* 1 tablespoon brown sugar
* 2 teaspoon salt
* ⅛ teaspoon ground black pepper
* 1 ½ teaspoon ground cumin
* 2 pounds skinless, boneless chicken thighs, cut into 1 ½" chunks (can use breast, but will not be as juicy)
* 2 (4.5 ounce) cans Red Gold Whole Peeled Tomatoes, drained
* 1 large red bell pepper, seeded and cut into 1 ½" pieces
* 1 large green bell pepper, seeded and cut into 1 ½" pieces
* 1 large sweet onion, peeled and cut into 1 ½" cubes

Directions:

1. To make the marinade, whisk together cilantro, lime juice, olive oil, garlic, sugar, salt,

black pepper and cumin in small bowl until well combined.

2. Place chicken cubes in large resealable plastic bag and pour in marinade. Remove as much air as possible and seal. Place in fridge for 1-5 hours.

3. Thread Flexible Skewers by alternating with chicken, tomato, peppers and onion until all ingredients are used.

4. Preheat the grill to 400°F using direct heat with a cast iron grate installed.

5. Place skewers on kamado grill and grill 3-4 minutes per side until chicken is cooked through and veggies have a nice char. Remove from heat and let rest 5 minutes before serving.

Greg Bates Bbq Chicken

Servings:8
Cooking Time: 30 Minutes

Ingredients:

- Trimmed chicken Breasts
- 2 cups Dr Pepper
- 2 cups ketchup
- ½ cup no-pulp orange juice
- ¼ cup Worcestershire sauce
- ¼ cup molasses
- 1 tsp ground ginger
- 1 tsp hot paprika
- 1 tsp chipotle Chile powder
- 2 tsp garlic powder
- 2 tsp onion powder
- ½ teaspoon crushed red pepper flakes

Directions:

1. Preheat the grill to 450°F using direct heat with a cast iron grate installed.

2. On your grill over medium high heat for 10 to 15 minutes on each side, brushing the Dr Pepper BBQ sauce on the chicken each time you turn it over. Grill until chicken is cooked through and juices run clear.

3. Mix the Dr Pepper, ketchup, orange juice, Worcestershire sauce and molasses in a saucepan. Season with paprika, ginger, garlic powder, red pepper flakes, chipotle powder and onion powder. Bring the sauce to a boil over high heat, proceed to reduce to medium-low heat and simmer for 15 minutes while stirring occasionally.

4. Use right away on your BBQ chicken, or store in your fridge for about a week! Enjoy.

Amusement Park Turkey Legs

Servings: 4
Cooking Time: 240 Minutes

Ingredients:

- 2 fresh turkey drumsticks
- 4 cups Turkey Brine
- 2 cups apple or cherry wood chips, soaked in water for 30 minutes

Directions:

1. Submerge drumsticks into the turkey brine for as few as 2 hours and as long as overnight.

2. Remove the drumsticks and discard the brine. Pat the turkey dry.

3. Grilling:

4. Preheat the grill to 250°F using direct heat with a cast iron grate installed. Add soaked, drained wood chips to the burning coals.

5. Put the plate setter in place and place the grid on top.

6. Place the turkey legs on the grid and close the dome for 3-4 hours or until the turkey registers 170°F.

7. Remove the drumsticks and pretend to walk around an amusement park or renaissance fair

Grill Glazed Sweet Asian Chicken Pan Grill

Servings:4
Cooking Time: 15 Minutes

Ingredients:

- 3 chicken breasts, cut into bite-size pieces
- 2 cups broccoli, cut into bite-size pieces
- 1 red bell pepper, cut into thin 1" strips
- 1 medium red onion, cut into thin 1" strips
- 1 yellow bell pepper, cut into thin 1" strips
- 1 tablespoon soy sauce
- 1/4 cup brown sugar
- 1/2 tablespoon Better Than Bouillon Chicken Base
- 1/2 teaspoon fresh ginger, finely chopped
- 1/4 cup water

Directions:

1. Preheat the grill to 450°F using direct heat with a cast iron grate installed.

2. In a bowl, mix soy sauce, brown sugar, Roasted Chicken Base, ginger and water.

3. Mix chicken and all vegetables in a Stir-Fry and Paella Pan. Place on the kamado grill.

4. Cook approximately 12-15 minutes or until chicken is thoroughly cooked and vegetables are soft.

5. Serve with rice or Asian noodles.

Bou Lentil Turkey Burgers

Servings:6
Cooking Time: 20 Minutes

Ingredients:

- 1 lb ground turkey (very cold)
- Red Split Lentils, prepared
- 1/2 tsp salt
- 1/2 tsp black pepper
- Bou Java Rub (optional for seasoning)
- 1/2 cup red split lentils (soaked for 3 hours)
- 1 BOU Beef or Chicken Broth Cube
- 1 cup water
- 2 BOU Chicken Bouillon Cubes
- 1/4 cup espresso coffee, finely ground
- 2 tbsp lemon zest, finely grated
- 1/2 cup brown sugar
- 2 tbsp sea salt
- 1 tbsp granulated garlic
- 1 1/2 tsp coriander, ground
- 3 tbsp chipotle chili powder
- 2 tbsp black pepper, freshly ground
- 3 tbsp smoked paprika
- 1 tsp roasted cumin, ground
- 1 1/2 tbsp unsweetened cocoa powder
- 1 tsp dry mustard
- 1 1/2 tbsp ancho chili powder

Directions:

1. Thoroughly combine all ingredients. Divide the mixture into 6 equal portions and form into 1/2 inch thick patties. If desired, season with BOU Java Rub.

2. Grill 6 minutes each side (remember, this is poultry – the internal temperature must get to 165°F).

3. Serve on a grilled whole wheat bun with Dijonnaise, lettuce, tomato and red onion.

4. Crumble the BOU cube in a sauce pan; add the water and blend with a whisk to mix the cube into the water. Add the soaked red lentils; bring to a boil. Lower to a simmer and cook for 4-5 minutes (lentils will be al dente). Pour into a bowl, cover and cool completely under refrigeration.

5. Combine all ingredients in a blender for about 45 seconds.

6. Place into a storage container with a lid; store in a cool dry place

Chicken & Dumplings

Servings: 4
Cooking Time: 95 Minutes

Ingredients:

- 1 Springer Mountain Farms whole chicken
- 2 quarts water
- 3 tsp salt
- ¼ tsp pepper
- 1 cup onion, chopped
- ½ cup celery, chopped
- 1 clove garlic, minced
- 8 oz. sour cream
- 2½ cups flour
- 3 eggs
- ½ cup water
- 2 tsp salt

Directions:

1. Preheat the grill to 325°F using direct heat with a cast iron grate installed.

2. Combine chicken, water, salt and pepper in dutch oven. Bring to a boil. Reduce heat; cover and simmer 1 hour. Remove chicken pieces; cut chicken into bite-size pieces, discarding skin and bones. Return chicken to broth along with onion, celery and garlic.

3. Cook 20 minutes. Add sour cream.

4. Combine flour, eggs (well beaten), water and 2 teaspoons salt and beat until batter is smooth. Drop batter by 1/2 teaspoon into boiling pot. Cover and simmer 15 minutes.

Wild Rice Turkey Biryani Stuffed Whole Pumpkin

Servings:12
Cooking Time: 40 Minutes

Ingredients:

- 1 large sugar pumpkin (approx. 3-4 pounds)
- 6 tbsp clarified butter
- 2 sweet onions, chopped
- 3 cloves garlic, minced
- 1 tsp fresh ginger, minced
- 10 green cardamom pods
- 3 whole cinnamon sticks
- ¼ tsp ground cloves
- ¼ tsp chili powder
- 1 tsp ground cumin
- 1 tsp ground coriander
- ½ tsp ground black pepper
- 1 cup wild rice
- 1 cup basmati rice, rinsed until clear water
- 2 lbs. ground turkey or chicken, cooked and browned
- 1 lemon
- 1 cup Craisins
- 1 cup tart apple (Granny Smith), diced
- ¾ cup pecans, toasted and chopped
- Coconut Oil
- Dizzy Pig Curry-ish
- 4 cups water

Directions:

1. Prepare Pumpkin:

2. Wash and dry the pumpkin.

3. Slice the top off the pumpkin using a sharp knife.

4. Remove the seeds and stringy center. Save the seeds for later.

5. Rub the inside of the pumpkin with melted coconut oil and Dizzy Pig Curry-ish.

6. Prepare Biryani (can be made a day ahead):

7. Melt the butter in a dutch oven.

8. Add the chopped onion and cook until browned.

9. Add garlic and ginger and next 7 ingredients. Saute until the spices "bloom", but careful not to burn.

10. Add the wild rice and basmati rice and mix well.

11. Add the water to the rice mixture and bring to a boil, cover and simmer for 30 minutes or until all of the liquid has been absorbed. Remove from heat.

12. Remove cinnamon sticks and cardamom pods from mixture.

13. Add the turkey, juice of 1 lemon, Craisins, apple and pecans.

14. Prepare Egg & Pumpkin:

15. Preheat the grill to 325°F using direct heat with a cast iron grate installed.

16. Place pumpkin in a pie plate.

17. Fill pumpkin to top with Biryani and place pumpkin lid on top.

18. Place pumpkin in pie plate on the platesetter – preferable to use the egg "feet" to raise it off the platesetter, but can be put directly on it.

19. Close lid of the egg and be sure that the stem of the pumpkin clears the hole on the Egg lid and that the temperature gauge does not pierce the flesh of the Egg.

20. Roast the pumpkin for 40 minutes or until a toothpick or knife can be inserted with minimal resistance. It should be the consistency of a cooked baked potato.

21. Remove from Egg and allow to rest with the top on for at least 10 minutes.

22. To Serve:

23. Scoop out the Biryani, ensuring to scoop the roasted pumpkin in the serving. Enjoy!

Hoisin Glazed Wings

Servings: 4
Cooking Time: 30 Minutes

Ingredients:
- 3-4 lbs chicken wings
- 1 cup Chinese Barbecue Sauce
- 1/4 cup Asian Rub

Directions:
1. Liberally dust the wings with the Asian Rub. Set aside.
2. Grilling:
3. Preheat the grill to 400°F using direct heat with a cast iron grate installed.
4. Place the wings on the grid with the dome closed for 20-30 minutes, turning once halfway through cooking.
5. When the juices run clear, place the wings in a large bowl and pour the Chinese Barbecue Sauce Sauce over them. Toss to coat.
6. Replace the wings on the grid and close all of the vents. Allow the wings to finish for 5 minutes.
7. Toss in the sauce once more and serve.

Peking Duck

Servings: 6
Cooking Time: 250 Minutes

Ingredients:
- 1 (5 lb) duck
- 1/4 cup Asian Rub
- 1 cup Chinese Barbecue Sauce (optional)

Directions:
1. Pat the duck dry.
2. Score the duck skin in one direction, then the other so you end up with a diamond pattern on the skin. (Scoring means you only cut through the skin, not the fat or meat.)
3. Liberally season all sides and the cavity with Asian Rub.

4. Allow the duck to rest in the fridge for 1 hour, bringing it back to room temperature while the grill preheats.

5. Grilling:

6. Preheat the grill to 300°F using direct heat with a cast iron grate installed, placing the plate setter and grids inside.

7. Place the duck, breast side up, on a rack, in a roasting pan that will fit inside the grill. The duck will render about 1 1/2 cups of fat.

8. Place the roasting rack inside the grill and close the dome for 1 hour.

9. Flip the duck back side up and close the dome for 1 hour.

10. Flip the duck breast side up and close the dome for 1 hour.

11. Finally, flip the duck back side up and close the dome for 1 hour.

12. Baste the duck with Chinese Barbecue Sauce (if desired). Adjust the temperature to 400°F. Close the dome for a final 5-7 minutes to crisp the skin, and remove.

13. Allow to sit uncovered for 10 minutes before carving.

14. Substitute duck fat for olive oil when cooking potatoes, root vegetables, or even eggs. Once rendered, strain the fat of any solids and save it in an airtight container in the fridge for up to 1 week.

Country Chicken Saltimbocca

Servings:8

Cooking Time: 30 Minutes

Ingredients:

- 3 6-8 oz (170-225 g) chicken breasts
- 4 cups (960 ml) cleaned and destemmed collard greens
- 6 slices cooked Applewood-smoked bacon, crumbled
- 2 tbsp (30 ml) extra virgin olive oil
- 2 cloves garlic, minced
- 3 slices aged cheddar cheese
- 1 tbsp (15 ml) garlic powder
- 1 tbsp (15 ml) onion powder
- 1 tsp (5 ml) white pepper
- 1 tbsp (15 ml) seasoning salt
- 4 tbsp (60 ml) butter
- 4 tbsp (60 ml) flour
- 2 cups (480 ml) half-and-half
- Reserved liquid from chicken
- 1 tbsp (15 ml) smoked paprika
- 6 leaves of basil

Directions:

1. Preheat the grill to 350°F using direct heat with a cast iron grate installed.

2. Pound chicken breasts until ¼ inch thick. Coat chicken breasts with ¾ of the seasoning mix; set aside.

3. Chiffonade collard greens into strips no wider than ¼ inch. Heat a Cast Iron Skillet with the olive oil. Add greens, then garlic and the remaining seasoning mix, cooking until wilted, 5-7 minutes.

4. Lay out the chicken breasts with the interior side up. Layer each in the following order: one slice of cheese, 1/3 of the bacon crumbles, 1/3 of the cooked collards. The bacon and collards should be placed in a thin even layer across the whole breast. Beginning at the short tapered end, roll up each chicken breast as you would for a jellyroll. Secure with a toothpick.

5.   Place rolls in a Roasting & Drip Pan, evenly spaced with room between each roll.

6.   Place the pan on the grid and bake for 15 to 20 minutes or until the chicken is firm. Remove from the kamado grill and allow to rest for at least 5 minutes. Remove the chicken from the pan; reserve the liquid for the sauce.

7.   Remove the platesetter and grill each side of the chicken for 1 minute for color and added flavor. Gently slice each into pinwheels, no less than ½ inch wide. Top with sauce and serve.

8.   Mix all seasoning ingredients together and set aside.

9.   Melt butter in a sauce pan. Whisk flour into butter. Cook for 90 seconds once incorporated, continuously whisking. Slowly add half-and-half, whisking in each addition until incorporated in flour mix. Season to taste. Add the reserved chicken liquid the same way. Add smoked paprika and cook at a low simmer for 2 minutes, or until it's at the thickness you desire; remove from heat. Chiffonade basil, add to warm sauce just before serving.

DESSERTS

Grilled Plums With Honey And Ricotta

Servings: 4
Cooking Time: 5 Minutes

Ingredients:
- 4 plums, cut in half and pitted
- 1/2 cup whole milk ricotta cheese
- 2 Tablespoons honey
- 1/4 tsp cracked black pepper

Directions:
1. Place the plums, cut side down on a 400°F grill.
2. Close the dome for 5 minutes.
3. Assembly:
4. Serve the plums, cut side up, with a dollop of ricotta, a drizzle of honey, and a sprinkling of cracked black pepper.

Brownies

Servings: 6
Cooking Time: 30 Minutes

Ingredients:
- 1 1/2 cups flour
- 1 cup white sugar
- 1 cup brown sugar
- 3/4 cups cocoa powder
- 1/2 cup butter, melted
- 1/4 cup vegetable oil
- 2 tsp vanilla
- 1 tsp baking powder
- 1/2 tsp salt
- 4 eggs
- 1/2 cup chocolate chips
- 1/2 chip marshmallows

Directions:
1. In a large bowl, combine butter, oil and sugars.
2. Add eggs, one at a time, stirring in between.
3. Add vanilla and stir.
4. Sift together cocoa powder, baking powder, and flour.
5. Add to the butter and egg mixture and stir until just combined.
6. Grilling:
7. Preheat the grill to 350°F using direct heat with a cast iron grate installed.
8. Line the dutch oven with a liner.
9. Pour the batter into the liner.
10. Cover the dutch oven, place on the grid, and lower the dome for 25-30 minutes or until a toothpick inserted into the middle comes out clean.
11. Remove the lid, top the brownies with chocolate chips and marshmallows and replace the lid for 5 minutes until the toppings are melted.

Caramel Cinnamon Rolls

Servings: 4
Cooking Time: 30 Minutes

Ingredients:
- 18 frozen cinnamon rolls, thawed (you can also used canned cinnamon rolls)
- 1/2 cup brown sugar
- 1/2 cup graham cracker crumbs
- 1/2 cup caramel ice cream topping
- 1 tsp cinnamon

Directions:
1. Line the dutch oven with a liner.

2. Cut each cinnamon roll into 4 pieces and arrange them around the bottom of the dutch oven.

3. In a separate bowl, combine brown sugar, graham cracker crumbs, and cinnamon.

4. Sprinkle some of the mixture over the layer of cinnamon rolls. Repeat.

5. Grilling:

6. Preheat the grill to 350°F using direct heat with a cast iron grate installed.

7. Cover the dutch oven and place it on the grid of the grill.

8. Lower the dome for 25-30 minutes or until the cinnamon rolls are golden brown.

9. Drizzle caramel ice cream topping over the warm rolls and serve.

Upside Down Triple Berry Pie

Servings: 8
Cooking Time: 35 Minutes

Ingredients:
- 6 cups frozen triple berry mix
- 2 Tablespoons lemon juice
- 1 refrigerated pie crust
- 1 cup sugar, divided
- 4 Tablespoons cornstarch

Directions:
1. Place a liner in the dutch oven.
2. In a separate bowl, combine frozen berries with 3/4 cup sugar, cornstarch, and lemon juice.
3. Pour berries into the bottom of the lined dutch oven.
4. Unroll pie crust and place on top of berry mixture.
5. Cut 4 vent holes into the crust.
6. Sprinkle remaining sugar over the pie crust.
7. Grilling:

8. Preheat the grill to 425°F using direct heat with a cast iron grate installed.

9. Cover the dutch oven and place on the grid.

10. Lower the dome for 35 minutes or until the crust is golden and the berry mixture has thickened.

11. Cut the crust as you would any pie.

12. Serve a piece of crust topped with ice cream and a scoop of the thickened berry mixture.

Berry Upside-down Cake

Servings: 10
Cooking Time: 30 Minutes

Ingredients:
- 10 tbsp unsalted butter, at room temperature, divided
- 1 cup packed light brown sugar, divided
- 11oz (315g) fresh seasonal berries
- 1 large egg
- 1 tsp pure vanilla extract
- 2⁄3 cup sour cream
- 11⁄3 cups all-purpose flour
- 1 tbsp baking powder
- 1⁄4 tsp baking soda
- 1⁄2 tsp kosher salt
- 1⁄4 tsp ground cinnamon
- fresh mint leaves, to garnish
- whipped cream, to serve

Directions:
1. Preheat the grill to 350°F (177°C) using indirect heat with a standard grate installed and a cast iron skillet on the grate. Melt 2 tbsp butter in the skillet and swirl to coat. Remove the skillet from the grill. Sprinkle 1⁄3 cup brown sugar over butter, pour in berries, and shake the skillet until berries are evenly spread out. Set aside.

2. In the bowl of a stand mixer fitted with the paddle attachment, cream together remaining 8

tbsp butter and 2/3 cup brown sugar until fluffy. Add egg, vanilla, and sour cream, and beat to combine.

3. In a medium bowl, sift together flour, baking powder, baking soda, salt, and cinnamon. Gradually add the dry ingredients to the butter and egg mixture until just incorporated. (The batter will be thick.) Using a rubber spatula, scoop the batter into the skillet, smoothing it over berries.

4. Place the skillet on the grate, close the lid, and bake until golden brown and a cake tester inserted into the middle of the cake comes out clean, about 30 minutes. Remove the skillet from the grill and place on a wire rack to cool for 15 minutes.

5. To serve, flip the cake upside down on a large serving platter and release from the skillet, leaving the berries on top. Garnish with fresh mint leaves, and serve with a dollop of whipped cream.

Grilled Sopapillas

Servings: 6
Cooking Time: 18 Minutes

Ingredients:
- 1 pizza dough, divided into 6 pieces
- 3 Tablespoons melted butter
- 1/4 cup sugar
- 1 Tablespoon cinnamon

Directions:
1. Stretch dough into round shape.
2. Place the dough directly on the pizza stone in a 500°F grill.
3. Brush with melted butter and top with cinnamon sugar.
4. Close the dome for 3 minutes, then remove.
5. Repeat with remaining dough.

4 Ingredient, No Knead Bread

Servings: 4
Cooking Time: 30 Minutes

Ingredients:
- 3 cups warm water
- 1 1/2 Tablespoons yeast
- 1 1/2 Tablespoons salt
- 6 1/2 cups bread flour

Directions:
1. In a 4-quart ice cream container, mix all ingredients until they come together. DO NOT KNEAD.
2. Cover, but do not seal the container and allow it to sit in a warm, dry place until it doubles in size, about 30 minutes.
3. Seal the container and place in the fridge for 1 hour.
4. Place a sheet of parchment paper in the bottom of the dutch oven.
5. Pinch off 1/4 of the dough and form into a ball.
6. Place the ball on the parchment paper and allow it to rest while the grill heats.
7. Grilling:
8. Preheat the grill to 425°F using direct heat with a cast iron grate installed.
9. Score the top of the dough ball with an "X".
10. Cover the dutch oven and place it on the grid of the grill.
11. Lower the Dome for 30 minutes.
12. Remove the bread from the dutch oven and allow it to cool before slicing.

Death By Chocolate

Servings: 8
Cooking Time: 60 Minutes

Ingredients:
- 1 chocolate cake mix, prepared according to package directions
- 2 cups chocolate chips
- 1 cup brown sugar
- 1 1/2 cups water
- 1/2 cup cocoa powder
- 1 (10 oz) bag miniature marshmallows

Directions:
1. Prepare cake mix according to package instructions.
2. Line the dutch oven with a liner.
3. In a medium bowl, combine water, brown sugar, and cocoa powder.
4. Pour the mixture into the bottom of the dutch oven.
5. Top with miniature marshmallows
6. Pour prepared cake mix on top.
7. Top with chocolate chips.
8. Grilling:
9. Preheat the grill to 350°F using direct heat with a cast iron grate installed.
10. Place the lid on the dutch oven and set on the grid of the grill.
11. Close the dome for 1 hour.
12. Remove the dutch oven from the grill, uncover, and serve warm.

3 Ingredient Fruit Cobbler

Servings: 8
Cooking Time: 30 Minutes

Ingredients:
- 1 stick butter, sliced
- 2 (29 oz) cans fruit, drained but reserving 1/2 cup of the liquid
- 1 yellow cake mix

Directions:
1. Line the dutch oven with a liner
2. Pour fruit into the bottom of the dutch oven with 1/2 cup of reserved liquid
3. Sprinkle the top with cake mix
4. Dot the top with butter.
5. Grilling:
6. Preheat the grill to 350°F using direct heat with a cast iron grate installed.
7. Cover the dutch oven and place on the grid of the grill.
8. Lower the dome for 30 minutes.
9. Allow the cobbler to sit for 10 minutes off the heat before serving.

Chocolate Cake

Servings: 12
Cooking Time: 45 Minutes

Ingredients:
- 2 cups all-purpose flour
- 2 cups sugar
- 2/3 cup cocoa powder
- 2 tsp baking soda
- 1 tsp baking powder
- 1 tsp kosher salt
- 2 large eggs, at room temperature
- 1 cup buttermilk, at room temperature
- 1 cup strong black coffee, warm
- 1/2 cup vegetable oil
- 1 tbsp pure vanilla extract
- flaky sea salt, for topping (optional)
- for the caramel sauce
- 3/4 cup sugar
- 4 tbsp water
- 4 tsp light corn syrup

- 1/4 cup heavy cream
- 1 tsp pure vanilla extract
- 11/2 tbsp unsalted butter
- for the frosting
- 12 tbsp unsalted butter, at room temperature
- 21/2 cups powdered sugar
- 1 tsp pure vanilla extract
- 1 tbsp heavy cream
- kosher salt

Directions:

1. Preheat the grill to 350°F (177°C) using indirect heat with a standard grate installed. Grease a 9-in (23-cm) round metal cake pan with nonstick cooking spray and line with parchment paper. (Instead of a cake pan, you can also use a well-seasoned dutch oven.)

2. In a large bowl or the bowl of a stand mixer, sift together flour, sugar, cocoa powder, baking soda, baking powder, and salt. In a separate medium bowl, whisk together eggs, buttermilk, coffee, vegetable oil, and vanilla extract.

3. Gradually add the liquid ingredients to the dry ingredients, stopping to scrape the sides and bottom of the bowl, until just combined. (The batter will be thin.) Pour the batter into the prepared cake pan or dutch oven. Place on the grate, close the grill lid, and bake until a toothpick inserted in the center comes out almost clean, about 25 to 30 minutes. Let sit for 5 minutes, then turn out onto a wire rack to cool completely. (Use a butter knife to loosen the edges if needed.)

4. To make the caramel sauce, in a small saucepan, combine sugar, water, and corn syrup. Place on the stovetop over medium heat, and simmer until the mixture is deep amber in color, about 10 to 15 minutes. Slowly and carefully, add heavy cream, whisking constantly, then whisk in vanilla, butter, and a pinch of salt.

5. To make the frosting, in the bowl of a stand mixer fitted with the paddle attachment, beat butter on medium speed until light and fluffy, about 2 to 3 minutes. Add sugar, vanilla extract, heavy cream, and a pinch of salt. Beat on low speed until combined, about 1 minute. Increase the speed to medium-high and beat for 6 minutes. Add 1/2 cup caramel sauce and mix until combined.

6. Spread the frosting evenly over top and sides of the cooled cake, and drizzle with caramel sauce. Sprinkle with flaky sea salt (if desired) before serving.

Peach Dutch Baby

Servings: 8
Cooking Time: 25 Minutes

Ingredients:

- 8 oz frozen peaches, thawed (or 3 ripe peaches, peeled and sliced)
- 1 cup whole milk
- 4 eggs
- 1 cup flour
- 1/4 cup sugar
- 1/4 cup butter
- 1 tsp vanilla
- 1 tsp cinnamon
- 1/2 tsp salt

Directions:

1. In a blender, combine milk, flour, sugar, vanilla, cinnamon, salt, and eggs until smooth.

2. Grilling:

3. Preheat the grill to 425°F using direct heat with a cast iron grate installed.

4. Place the dutch oven on the grid of the grill and melt the butter.

5. Line the bottom of the pot with peaches and pour over milk and egg mixture.

6. Close the dome for 20 minutes or until the top of the Dutch Baby is golden brown.

7. Serve with a sprinkling of powdered sugar.

Fresh Peach Crisp

Servings: 4
Cooking Time: 5 Minutes

Ingredients:
- 2 peaches, halved with pits removed
- Vanilla Ice Cream
- 1 cup good quality granola

Directions:
1. Grilling:
2. Place the peach halves, cut side down, on a 400°F grill and cover with the dome for 5 minutes.
3. Assembly:
4. Remove the peaches and place them, cut side up, in a bowl. Top with vanilla ice cream and granola.

Chocolate Chip Cookie Peanut Butter Cup S'mores

Servings: 4
Cooking Time: 5 Minutes

Ingredients:
- 8 chocolate chip cookies
- 4 peanut butter cup candies
- 4 marshmallows

Directions:
1. On the grid of a 225°F grill, place one cookie, flat side up, with one peanut butter cup candy and one marshmallow on top.
2. Close the dome for 5 minutes or until the marshmallow begins to puff.

3. Assembly:
4. Close the s'more with the other chocolate chip cookie and get ready for the sugar rush.

Apple Pizza

Servings: 8
Cooking Time: 5 Minutes

Ingredients:
- 1 pizza dough
- 1 cup apple pie filling
- 1/4 cup vanilla cake mix
- 2 Tablespoon melted butter
- Vanilla Ice Cream

Directions:
1. Stretch pizza dough into a 14" round and place on a pizza peel.
2. In a small bowl, combine cake mix and melted butter until it forms a crumbly texture.
3. Spread apple pie filling over pizza dough and top with crumb mixture.
4. Grilling:
5. Bake on a pizza stone in a 500°F grill for 5 minutes.
6. Slice and serve with vanilla frosting.

Orange Scented Vanilla Cake

Servings: 12
Cooking Time: 30 Minutes

Ingredients:
- 12 oranges
- 1/2 stick of butter
- 1 vanilla cake mix, prepared according to package instructions
- 1/2 lb of powdered sugar

Directions:
1. Cut the tops off of the oranges and, using a spoon, scoop out the insides of the orange. Eat

the insides of the orange while you wait for the cake to cook.

2. Pour 1/3 of a cup of batter into each orange, replace the top and wrap with heavy duty aluminum foil.

3. In a separate bowl, combine butter, powdered sugar, and 2 Tablespoon orange juice.

4. When cakes are ready, drizzle some of the glaze over top of each cake and serve inside the orange.

5. Grilling:

6. Place the oranges on a 350°F grill for 30 minutes or until the cake is done.

Grilled Watermelon With Honey Yogurt

Servings: 4
Cooking Time: 4 Minutes

Ingredients:

- 1 round of watermelon, 1 inch thick
- 1/2 cup Greek-style yogurt
- 1 Tablespoon honey
- 1/4 tsp vanilla

Directions:

1. Place the watermelon on a 400°F grill with the dome down for 1 minute.

2. Turn the watermelon and lower the dome for an additional minute.

3. Assembly:

4. Cut the watermelon in quarters and place each on a small plate.

5. In a small bowl, combine yogurt, honey, and vanilla and spoon equal amounts over the watermelon. Serve.

Grilled Pineapple Sundaes

Servings: 4

Cooking Time: 5 Minutes

Ingredients:

- 4 fresh pineapple spears
- Vanilla Ice Cream
- Jarred Caramel Sauce
- Toasted Coconut

Directions:

1. Place pineapple spears on a 400°F grill and close the dome for 2 minutes.

2. Turn the pineapple and close the dome for another 2 minutes.

3. Turn the pineapple once more and close the dome for another minute.

4. Assembly:

5. Serve pineapple topped with ice cream, caramel sauce, and toasted coconut.

Best Banana Bread

Servings: 6
Cooking Time: 40 Minutes

Ingredients:

- 1 cup plain yogurt
- 1/4 cup butter
- 3 very ripe bananas, peeled
- 2 eggs
- 2 cups flour
- 2/3 cups sugar
- 3/4 tsp salt
- 1/2 tsp vanilla extract
- 1/2 tsp baking soda
- 1/4 tsp baking powder

Directions:

1. In a blender, combine bananas, yogurt, sugar, butter, vanilla, and eggs until smooth.

2. In a large bowl, sift together flour, salt, baking powder, and baking soda.

3. Gradually add the wet ingredients into the dry ingredients and gently stir to combine. DO NOT OVER MIX.

4. Line a dutch oven with a liner.

5. Pour batter into the dutch oven and cover.

6. Grilling:

7. Preheat the grill to 350°F using direct heat with a cast iron grate installed and place the dutch oven on the grid.

8. Lower the dome for 30 minutes or until a toothpick inserted into the center comes out clean.

Peaches And Pound Cake

Servings: 6
Cooking Time: 5 Minutes

Ingredients:
- 1/2 cup heavy whipping cream
- 2 Tablespoons sour cream
- 3 peaches, halved and pitted
- 1 store-bought pound cake, cut into 6 slices

Directions:
1. Place the peaches, cut side down, on a 400°F grill.

2. Place the pound cake slices alongside the peaches and close the dome for 2 minutes.

3. Flip the pound cake, and close the dome for an additional 2-3 minutes.

4. Assembly:

5. In a stand mixer, whip the whipping cream until stiff peaks form. Fold in the sour cream to combine.

6. Place a slice of pound cake on a plate, top with a peach half, and a dollop of the cream.

Triple Berry Crostata

Servings: 8
Cooking Time: 50 Minutes

Ingredients:
- 1 1/2 cups all-purpose flour
- 11 Tablespoons butter, cut into 1/2 inch cubes
- 3 Tablespoons whole milk
- 2 tsp sugar
- 1 large egg yolk
- 2 cups frozen triple berry blend
- 1/4 cup sugar
- 2 Tablespoons cornstarch

Directions:
1. In a food processor, combine flour and butter and pulse until pea-sized cubes of butter can be seen throughout the flour.

2. Add sugar, egg yolk, and milk and pulse until the dough comes together.

3. Form the dough into a circle, cover tightly with plastic wrap, and refrigerate 20 minutes.

4. Roll the dough into a large round and place on a pizza peel covered in cornmeal.

5. In a bowl, combine fruit, sugar, and cornstarch and pile into the center of the dough.

6. Beginning on one side, fold the dough 1/3 of the way over the fruit, repeating until a free-form tart is formed.

7. Grilling:

8. Preheat the grill to 350°F using direct heat with a cast iron grate installed.

9. Slide the crostata onto the pizza stone and close the dome for 40-55 minutes or until the crust is golden brown.

10. Remove the crostata from the grill and allow to cool slightly before slicing and serving.

Almond Cream Cake

Servings: 16
Cooking Time: 45 Minutes

Ingredients:

- 2 cups butter, softened
- 3 cups sugar
- 6 cups cake flour
- 1 tsp kosher salt
- 4 tsp baking powder
- 2 cups whole milk
- 2 tsp almond extract
- 10 large eggs, whites only
- sliced almonds, to decorate
- for the frosting
- 1¼ cups all-purpose flour
- 2 cups whole milk
- ½ tsp almond extract
- 1 tbsp vanilla bean paste
- 2 cups butter, softened
- 2 cups sugar

Directions:

1. In the bowl of a stand mixer fitted with the paddle attachment, cream butter until white in appearance. Add sugar and beat until fluffy. In a large bowl, sift together flour, salt, and baking powder. Add the flour mixture to the butter mixture in three stages, alternating with the milk and almond extract and mixing after each addition until just combined.

2. In a large bowl, beat egg whites until they form stiff peaks. Using a spatula, gently fold egg whites into the cake batter, taking care not to overmix.

3. Preheat the grill to 350°F (177°C) using indirect heat with a standard grate installed. Line an 11 x18-in (28 x 46cm) grill-safe baking pan with parchment paper and lightly grease with cooking spray. Pour the batter into the pan, place on the grate, close the lid, and bake until the top springs back when touched, about 27 to 30 minutes.

4. Remove the cake from the grill and place on a wire rack to cool for 10 minutes. Use a knife to loosen the edges, and transfer the cake to a wire rack to cool completely.

5. To make the frosting, on the stovetop in a saucepan over medium-low heat, whisk together flour and milk until mixture thickens to the consistency of mashed potatoes, about 12 to 15 minutes. Stir constantly, and lower the heat if needed. Remove the saucepan from the heat and place in a bowl of ice for 5 to 10 minutes to hasten the cooling process and bring the mixture to room temperature. Once cool, stir in almond extract.

6. In the bowl of a stand mixer, cream together vanilla paste, butter, and sugar until the mixture is light and fluffy and sugar is completely dissolved. Add the flour mixture, and beat until it has the appearance of whipped cream, scraping the sides of the bowl as needed.

7. Spread the frosting evenly over the cooled cake and sprinkle sliced almonds over top to decorate before serving.

Whole Apples With Caramel Sauce

Servings: 4
Cooking Time: 60 Minutes

Ingredients:

- 4 Jonathan Apples
- 1 cup packed dark brown sugar
- 1/2 cup half and half
- 4 Tablespoons butter
- 1 tsp vanilla extract

Directions:

1. In a medium saucepan, whisk together the brown sugar, butter, and half and half until melted.

2. Continue whisking 5-7 minutes until the caramel begins to thicken.

3. Add vanilla and set aside to cool before storing in a jar in the fridge.

4. Using a melon baller, scoop the core from the apple.

5. Wrap each apple in aluminum foil.

6. Grilling:

7. Preheat the grill to 225°F using direct heat with a cast iron grate installed for 1 hour.

8. Remove apples from the grill, serve topped with caramel sauce.

Peanut Butter Bacon Bars

Servings: 8
Cooking Time: 25 Minutes

Ingredients:

- 1 package peanut butter cookie mix
- 1/2 cup chopped peanuts
- 1/2 cup bacon, cooked and crumbled
- 1/3 cup vegetable oil
- 1 egg
- 1 cup semi-sweet chocolate chips
- 1/2 cup bacon, cooked and crumbled

Directions:

1. Combine cookie mix, vegetable oil, egg, bacon, and peanuts and press into a lined dutch oven.

2. Grilling:

3. Preheat the grill to 350°F using direct heat with a cast iron grate installed.

4. Cover the dutch oven and place on the grid.

5. Lower the dome for 25 minutes.

6. Remove the lid and top with chocolate chips.

7. Replace the cover for 5 minutes until the chocolate chips are melted.

8. Spread the chocolate over the bars to coat them evenly.

9. Top with remaining bacon.

10. Allow the bars to cool before cutting.

Banana Boats

Servings: 4
Cooking Time: 10 Minutes

Ingredients:

- 4 green bananas
- Chocolate chips
- Miniature marshmallows
- Peanut butter chips
- Crushed cookies

Directions:

1. Split a banana lengthwise from end to end leaving the peel intact on the opposite side.

2. Top with desired toppings.

3. Wrap the banana in heavy duty aluminum foil.

4. Grilling:

5. Preheat the grill to 425°F using direct heat with a cast iron grate installed and close the dome for 10 minutes.

6. Unwrap and serve topped with vanilla ice cream, whipped cream, or by themselves

S'mores Pizza

Servings: 8
Cooking Time: 5 Minutes

Ingredients:

- 1 pizza dough
- 1/2 cup semi-sweet chocolate chips
- 1/2 cup miniature marshmallows
- 1/4 cup slightly crushed graham crackers

Directions:

1. Stretch dough to a 14" round and place on a pizza peel.
2. Sprinkle dough with chocolate chips, miniature marshmallows, and graham cracker crumbs.
3. Grilling:
4. Slide the pizza onto the prepared stone at 500°F.
5. Cook for 5 minutes, remove from the stone, slice, and serve.

Sourdough Baguette

Servings: 4
Cooking Time: 25 Minutes

Ingredients:

- cornmeal, for dusting
- for Day 1 (starter)
- 8oz (225g) whole rye flour
- 8oz (235ml) warm water (105°F [41°C])
- for Day 2
- 8oz (225g) bread flour
- for Day 3
- 12oz (340g) bread flour
- 6oz (177ml) warm water (105°F [41°C])
- 8oz (225g) starter
- for Day 4
- 3oz (85g) whole rye flour
- 31oz (915ml) warm water (105°F [41°C])
- 9 1/2oz (270g) starter
- 42oz (1.2kg) bread flour
- 3oz (85g) whole wheat flour
- 1oz (25g) kosher salt

Directions:

1. On Day 1, in a large bowl, combine flour and water, cover tightly with plastic wrap, and let sit overnight on the counter at warm room temperature, about 70°F (21°C). (Cooler temperatures might inhibit the growth of the starter.)
2. On Day 2, add flour to the starter and mix until a stiff, thick dough forms. Cover tightly with plastic wrap and let sit overnight on the counter at warm room temperature. The dough will rise overnight.
3. On Day 3, in a large bowl, combine flour, water, and 8 ounces (225g) of the starter, and mix until a stiff, thick dough forms. Cover tightly with plastic wrap and let sit overnight on the counter at warm room temperature. The dough will rise overnight and should begin to smell yeasty. (Freeze remaining starter for later use.)
4. On Day 4, preheat the grill to 400°F (204°C) using indirect heat with a standard grate installed and a pizza stone on the grate. In a large bowl, combine rye flour, water, 9 1/2 ounces (270g) of the starter, bread flour, wheat flour, and salt, and mix until a dough forms. Cover tightly with plastic wrap and let sit for 20 minutes on the counter. The dough will continue to smell yeasty. (Freeze remaining starter for later use.)
5. Form the dough into 4 baguette shapes that are 10 to 12 inches (25cm to 30.5cm) long and about 2 1/2 inches (6.25cm) around. Make 3 slits in the top of each loaf to allow steam to escape. Sprinkle the pizza stone with cornmeal and place the loaves on the pizza stone. Close the lid and bake until the bread reaches an internal temperature of 190°F (88°C), about 20 to 25 minutes.
6. Remove the baguettes from the grill, place on a cutting board, and let rest before slicing and serving as desired.

Buttermilk Biscuits

Servings: 6
Cooking Time: 15 Minutes

Ingredients:

- 3/4 cups buttermilk
- 1/2 cup butter, cut into 1/2 inch cubes
- 3 cups flour
- 1 1/2 tsp baking powder
- 1/2 tsp salt

Directions:

1. In the bowl of a food processor, combine flour, baking powder, salt and butter and pulse until the butter is the size of small peas.

2. With the food processor going, stream in buttermilk until the dough just comes together.

3. Turn out on a floured surface.

4. Pat the dough to 1/2-inch thickness and fold in half.

5. Pat the dough to 1/2-inch thickness and fold in half again.

6. Pat the dough a third time to 1/2-inch thickness.

7. Using a pizza cutter, cut the dough into 12 square biscuits.

8. Place a sheet of parchment in the bottom of the dutch oven.

9. Place biscuits on the bottom of the dutch oven, being careful that they do not touch. (You may have to do this in two batches.)

10. Grilling:

11. Preheat the grill to 425°F using direct heat with a cast iron grate installed.

12. Cover the dutch oven with the lid and place on the grid.

13. Lower the dome for 12-15 minutes.

14. Biscuits are done when they are golden brown. Serve with butter, honey, or jam.

Corn & Jalapeño Focaccia

Servings: 8
Cooking Time: 40 Minutes

Ingredients:

- 2½ cups all-purpose or bread flour
- 1 tbsp kosher salt
- ½ tbsp instant dry yeast
- 1½ cups warm water (105°F [41°C])
- 3 tbsp extra virgin olive oil
- 3 jalapeño peppers, left whole
- 1 ear of corn, shucked
- for the butter
- 1 tbsp olive oil
- 2 tbsp unsalted butter
- 4 garlic cloves, minced
- 2 tsp dried oregano
- ½ tsp red pepper flakes
- kosher salt

Directions:

1. In a large bowl, combine flour, salt, yeast, and water. Cover tightly with plastic wrap, and set aside to rest for at least 8 hours and up to 24 hours. The dough will rise dramatically and fill the bowl.

2. Pour oil into a large cast iron skillet. Transfer the dough to the skillet, turning the dough to coat in oil. Press the dough around the skillet, flattening slightly and spreading to fill the entire bottom. Cover tightly with plastic wrap and let sit at room temperature for 2 hours.

3. After the first hour, preheat the grill to 425°F (218°C) using indirect heat with a standard grate installed. Place jalapeños and corn on the grate near the edges. Close the lid and grill until beginning to soften and char, about 10 to 12 minutes. Cut the kernels from the cob, and seed and dice jalapeños. Set aside.

4. After resting for 2 hours, the dough should mostly fill the skillet. Use your fingertips to firmly press the dough to the edges, popping any large bubbles that appear. Lift the dough at the edges and allow any air bubbles underneath to escape.

5. Evenly scatter corn and jalapeños over the dough, then push down until they're embedded in the dough. Place the skillet on the grate, close the grill lid, and bake until the top is golden brown and the bottom appears golden brown and crisp when lifted at the edge with a spatula, about 16 to 24 minutes.

6. To make the butter, on the stovetop in a small saucepan over medium-low heat, heat oil and butter until butter melts. Add garlic, oregano, and pepper flakes, and cook for 1 minute, stirring constantly. Transfer to a small bowl and season with salt to taste.

7. Transfer the focaccia to a cutting board and brush the butter over top. Allow to cool slightly, slice, and serve with any remaining butter.

Seasonal Fruit Cobbler

Servings: 12
Cooking Time: 90 Minutes

Ingredients:

- 2lb (1kg) seasonal fruit, washed, pitted (if needed), and sliced or halved if needed
- 1/2 tsp ground cinnamon
- 2 tsp cornstarch (for juicy fruits; omit for pears or apples)
- 4 tbsp butter, plus more for greasing
- 1/2 cup sugar, plus more for sprinkling
- 3/4 cup self-rising flour
- 3/4 cup whole milk
- whipped cream, to serve

Directions:

1. Preheat the grill to 350°F (177°C) using indirect heat with a standard grate installed. Place the fruit on the grate (or in a cast iron skillet if the fruit might fall through the grate), close the lid, and grill until beginning to soften and char, about 7 to 10 minutes. Remove fruit from the grill and place in a large bowl. Sprinkle cinnamon and cornstarch (if using) over fruit, and add a little sugar (if desired). Gently toss to coat and set aside.

2. Grease a 9-in (23-cm) grill-safe baking pan with butter. On the stovetop in a small saucepan, heat 4 tbsp butter over medium-low heat until beginning to brown, about 10 to 15 minutes.

3. In a medium bowl, whisk together butter, sugar, flour, and milk. Transfer fruit to the prepared baking pan and spread the batter evenly over top. Place the pan on the grate, close the lid, and bake until golden brown and bubbly, about 1 hour. In the last 10 minutes of cooking, sprinkle a light amount of sugar over top. Remove the cobbler from the grill, and serve warm with whipped cream on top.

Lemon Poppy Seed Cake

Servings: 10
Cooking Time: 45 Minutes

Ingredients:

- 1 tsp poppy seeds
- 2 lemons, zested and juiced
- 1 vanilla cake mix prepared according to package directions, substituting melted butter for oil and buttermilk for water
- 1 lb powdered sugar
- 4 ounces cream cheese
- 1 stick butter, softened
- 1/2 tsp vanilla
- 1/2 tsp lemon extract

- The juice and zest of 1 lemon

Directions:

1. Prepare cake mix according to package directions, substituting melted butter for the oil and buttermilk for the water.

2. Add the lemon zest, lemon juice, and poppy seeds.

3. Line the dutch oven with a liner.

4. Pour prepare cake mix into the liner and cover.

5. Grilling:

6. Preheat the grill to 350°F using direct heat with a cast iron grate installed.

7. Place the dutch oven on the grid and lower the dome for 30-40 minutes or until a toothpick inserted into the center comes out clean.

8. Meanwhile, combine glaze ingredients, adding milk to thin out the glaze if necessary.

9. Remove the cake from the grill and set aside to cool for 10 minutes before pouring glaze over the cake.

10. Serve warm.

Grilled Naan

Servings: 24
Cooking Time: 6 Minutes

Ingredients:

- 1 cup warm water (105°F [41°C])
- 1/4oz (7g) active dry yeast
- 1/4 cup sugar
- 3 tbsp whole milk
- 1 large egg, beaten
- 2 tsp kosher salt
- 201/4oz (575g) bread flour, plus more for kneading
- vegetable oil, for greasing
- 1/4 cup butter, melted

Directions:

1. In a large bowl, combine water and yeast. Let sit until frothy, about 10 minutes. Stir in sugar, milk, egg, salt, and flour to make a soft dough. Knead on a lightly floured surface until smooth.

2. Lightly oil a large bowl, place the dough in the bowl, and cover with a damp cloth. Let sit to rise until the dough has doubled in volume, about 1 hour.

3. Punch the dough down and divide it into 4 balls (about the size of golf balls). Cover with a towel and allow to rise until the balls have doubled in size, about 30 minutes.

4. Preheat the grill to 425°F (218°C) using direct heat with a cast iron grate installed. Use a rolling pin one ball of dough into a thin circle. Lightly oil the grate, place the circle of dough on the grate, close the lid, and bake until puffy and lightly browned, about 2 to 3 minutes. Brush the uncooked side with butter, then flip the dough over and brush the cooked side with butter. Cook until puffy and lightly browned, about 3 minutes more. Repeat the cooking process with the remaining dough. (You can also bake all 4 balls at the same time.)

5. Remove the naan from the grill and sprinkle with seasoning of choice (if desired). Serve warm.

Pizza Margherita

Servings: 2
Cooking Time: 6 Minutes

Ingredients:

- cornmeal, for dusting
- 1/4 cup marinara sauce
- 2oz (55g) fresh mozzarella, sliced
- 3 garlic cloves, thinly sliced
- 12–16 fresh basil leaves
- kosher salt and freshly ground black pepper
- grated Parmesan, to serve

- for the dough
- 12oz (340g) Italian 00 flour, plus more for dusting
- 4 tsp kosher salt
- 2 tsp instant dry yeast
- 6½oz (190ml) warm water (105°F [41°C])

Directions:

1. To make the dough, in a large bowl, whisk together flour, salt, and yeast until well combined. Add water, and use your hands to mix until no dry flour remains. Cover tightly with plastic wrap and allow to rise at room temperature for 2 to 4 hours. Turn the dough out onto a lightly floured surface and allow to sit at room temperature for 2 hours before baking.

2. Preheat the grill to 600°F (316°C) using indirect heat with a pizza stone resting directly on the heat deflector. (The pizza stone should be level with the grill rim.)

3. On a lightly floured work surface, roll out the dough to ¼ in (.5cm) thick and a 10-in (25cm) diameter. Lightly dust a pizza paddle or unrimmed baking sheet with cornmeal, and place the dough on top. Evenly spread the sauce over the dough, working from the center to the edges. Top with the sliced mozzarella and garlic.

4. Carefully slide the pizza from the paddle to the hot pizza stone. Close the lid and bake until the crust is golden brown and the cheese is melted and beginning to bubble, about 4 to 6 minutes.

5. Use the pizza paddle to remove the pizza from the grill. Scatter the basil leaves over top and sprinkle with salt, pepper, and Parmesan.

Nutella And Strawberry Pizza

Servings: 8
Cooking Time: 5 Minutes

Ingredients:
- 1 pizza dough
- 1/2 lb sliced strawberries
- 1/4 cup Nutella

Directions:

1. Stretch the pizza dough into a 14 inch round and place it on a pizza peel.

2. Spread the dough with the Nutella and top with strawberries.

3. Grilling:

4. Slide the pizza onto the prepared stone in a 500°F grill and cook for 5 minutes.

5. Remove from the stone with a pizza peel and slice into 8 pieces.

BEEF

Cranberry-marinated Rack Of Lamb

Servings:4
Cooking Time: 50 Minutes

Ingredients:

- 2 Australian lamb racks, frenched
- 1 cup pure cranberry or pomegranate juice
- 1 cup white or red wine
- ½ cup cranberries
- 1 sprig fresh rosemary
- 2 tablespoons olive oil
- Salt and freshly ground pepper, to taste
- Almond Wild Rice
- 4 ounces pure wild rice
- ½ cup sliced almonds
- 2 tablespoons chopped fresh oregano leaves
- Juice and grated zest of ½ orange

Directions:

1. Place racks of lamb in large, deep dish. Add juice, wine, cranberries, and rosemary. Cover and marinate 2-3 hours or overnight.

2. Preheat the grill to 400°F using direct heat with a cast iron grate installed.

3. Remove lamb from marinade, pat dry and season to taste. Place marinade in a saucepan and bring to a boil. Reduce heat and simmer until reduced to a thin glaze. Discard rosemary. Keep glaze warm.

4. Heat oil in a Cast Iron Skillet and sear lamb on all sides to brown. Remove the skillet from the grill; place the lamb racks on the grid and cook 8-10 minutes for medium rare or until cooked as desired. Allow to rest for a few minutes before slicing into individual chops.

5. For the rice, place rice in pan of cold, salted water, and bring to a boil. Cook for 10 minutes. Turn off heat, cover and allow to steam 20 minutes (rice will swell and curl). Return to a simmer and cook 10 minutes or until tender. Keep warm. Just before serving, toss through the almonds, oregano, orange juice and zest.

6. Toss the rice with the almonds, oregano, juice, and zest.

7. Tip: Cook the rice and marinate the lamb the day before. Heat rice through in the Cast Iron Skillet with a little water, stock or wine, and toss with the remaining ingredients just before serving.

Brisket Burnt Ends

Servings:8
Cooking Time: 120 Minutes

Ingredients:

- Full packer brisket
- Meat Church Holy Cow
- Kansas City Style Sweet & Smoky BBQ Sauce
- Your favorite clover honey

Directions:

1. Preheat the grill to 275°F using direct heat with a cast iron grate installed. I recommend a heavier smoking wood chunks for this cook such as oak, hickory, mesquite, or pecan.

2. Trim the excess fat and silver skin from the brisket. Also, remove any "hard" pieces of fat as they will not render off during the cooking process. Trim the fat off the bottom of the brisket leaving only ¼ in (6 mm) fat.

3. A brisket is comprised of two muscles; the point (the fat end) and the flat (the lean end). In

order to be able to cook brisket burnt ends you need to butcher the brisket a bit more than you would for a traditional packer. Therefore, after your traditional brisket butchering, you need to start to separate the flat form the point. Using a sharp boning knife expose the point meat so it can absorb smoke. You don't have to completely separate the muscles.

4. Place the brisket in the kamado grill fat-side down. When the meat reaches an internal temperature of 160°F, double wrap the brisket in non-waxed butcher paper or aluminum foil. The bark will have formed nicely by this point.

5. Continue to smoke the brisket until it reaches an internal temperature of 195°F. The brisket is not completely done at this point but we need to separate the point to make burnt ends. Unwrap the brisket and separate the point from the flat. Re-wrap the flat and return it to your grill. Continue to smoke it until the meat is "probe tender" which means when you probe it with an instant read thermometer there is no resistance. Think of a toothpick in a cake. Each piece of meat is different but this will likely be between an internal temperature around 203° F. Rest your brisket flat in a cooler for at least one hour.

6. Take the point and cut it into 1" cubes. Place the cubes in the aluminum pan. Season and toss the cubes with more Meat Church Holy Cow. Cover the cubes with Kansas City Style Sweet & Smoky BBQ sauce. Drizzle honey across the top. Finally, toss the cubes thoroughly to ensure they are completely covered. Return the pan to the grill and cook for another 1 – 2 hours or until all liquid has reduced and caramelized.

7. Allow to cool for a few minutes and enjoy immediately!

Aged Prime Rib

Servings: 8

Cooking Time: 120 Minutes

Ingredients:
- 2 tsp garlic salt
- 2 tsp onion salt
- 2 tsp kosher salt
- 1 tsp freshly ground black pepper
- 2 tsp dried rosemary
- 4lb (1.8kg) bone-in prime rib roast, aged for at least 28 days
- 3 garlic cloves, slivered
- 1/2 to 1 cup beef stock, as needed
- for the marrow butter
- 2 beef marrow bones, cut in half lengthwise at the butcher
- 1/2lb (225g) butter, softened
- 3/4 tsp chopped fresh flat-leaf parsley
- kosher salt and freshly ground black pepper
- to smoke
- hickory or oak wood chunks

Directions:

1. In a medium bowl, combine garlic salt, onion salt, kosher salt, pepper, and rosemary. Place roast in a baking dish and use a sharp knife to cut tiny slits every 2 inches (5cm), and insert the garlic slivers in the slits. Rub the roast with the spice mixture, cover with plastic wrap, and refrigerate for 24 hours.

2. Preheat the grill to 225°F (107°C). Once hot, add the wood chunks, install the heat deflector with a drip pan placed on top, and install a standard grate. Place roast and marrow bones on the grate, close the lid, and smoke until the internal temperature of the meat reaches 125°F (52°C), about 2 hours. Transfer roast to a large

platter, cover with aluminum foil, and set aside to rest.

3.   Remove the bones from the grill, and use a spoon to scrape the marrow from the bones into a medium bowl. To make the marrow butter, add butter and parsley to the marrow, and mix until well combined. Season with salt and pepper to taste. Set aside.

4.   Remove the drip pan from the grill and pour the drippings into a medium all-metal saucepan. Place the saucepan on the heat deflector, close the lid, and heat for10 minutes, adding beef stock as needed. Season with salt and pepper to taste.

5.   Place roast on a cutting board and slice. Serve immediately with the marrow butter and warm jus for dipping.

Smoked Beef Short Ribs

Servings:4
Cooking Time: 250 Minutes

Ingredients:
- 1 teaspoon garlic powder
- 1 teaspoon onion powder
- 1 teaspoon smoked Spanish paprika
- ½ teaspoon cayenne pepper
- ½ teaspoon dried thyme
- 4 pounds bone-in beef short ribs, cut 2 to 2½ inches thick
- 16 ounces lager beer
- 2 cups chicken stock
- 2 cups white balsamic vinegar
- 4 tablespoons salted butter, cubed
- 1 teaspoon garlic powder
- 1 teaspoon onion powder
- 1 teaspoon smoked Spanish paprika
- ½ teaspoon cayenne pepper
- ½ teaspoon dried thyme
- ½ teaspoon ground coriander
- 1 tablespoon kosher salt

Directions:

1.   Preheat the grill to 225°F using direct heat with a cast iron grate installed.

2.   Generously rub the short ribs with the spices.

3.   Place the hickory chips in a small bowl, cover with water and let soak for at least 1 hour. Drain and scatter over the preheated charcoal. Using barbecue mitts, place the grid in the grill.

4.   Place the ribs on the grid; close the dome of the grill. Let the ribs smoke 1½ to 2 hours. Once the short ribs have finished smoking, transfer the ribs to the baking dish.

5.   Using the Grill Gripper and barbecue mitts, carefully remove the grid and add the platesetter and replace the grid. Raise the internal temperature of the kamado grill to 375°F.

6.   Mix the beer and the chicken broth in a large bowl and set aside. Place the vinegar in a heavy-bottomed saucepan on the stove top over medium heat for about 15 minutes, or until the liquid has reduced by half.

7.   Pour the beef and chicken mixture over the ribs.

8.   Cover the dish tightly with aluminum foil; place in the preheated kamado grill for 2½ hours, or until the ribs are fork tender.

9.   Warm the reduced vinegar over low heat. Using a whisk, add the butter a little at a time, stirring constantly, until the butter is emulsified. Do not boil. Transfer the ribs to plates, top with the sauce and serve immediately.

10. Mix the garlic powder, onion powder, paprika, cayenne pepper, thyme, coriander and salt in a small bowl.

Fire Grilled Steak With Steakhouse Butter

Servings:4

Cooking Time: 20 Minutes

Ingredients:

- ½ cup (120 ml) butter, softened
- 2 tbsp (30 ml) finely minced shallot or red onion
- 1 clove of garlic, finely minced
- 1 tbsp (15 ml) finely minced parsley
- 1 tbsp (15 ml) finely minced fresh thyme
- 2 tbsp (30 ml) of your favorite vinegar
- A sprinkle or two of salt and lots of freshly ground pepper
- 4 thick New York strip loin, sirloin or ribeye steaks
- A sprinkle or two of sea salt and freshly ground pepper on each steak

Directions:

1. Stir all the ingredients together until thoroughly combined. Scoop the butter into a large resealable bag. Press the butter and form a thick log shape, roughly 4 inches (10 cm) long. Tightly roll up the bag, shaping the butter into a perfect round log. Refrigerate or freeze for several hours or overnight until the butter is firm enough to slice.

2. Preheat the grill to 600°F using direct heat with a cast iron grate installed. Just before you begin to cook the steaks, pat them dry and season them heavily with salt and pepper. Position the steaks on the grid at a 45° angle to the grid lines. After a few minutes, turn them 90° to get the perfect steakhouse grill marks. Flip and repeat. Continue cooking until the steaks reach the doneness you prefer. You may press the steaks with your finger to gauge doneness; they stiffen as they cook through. This will take some time to master but it's a skill worth cultivating!

3. Top each steak with a thick slice of steakhouse butter; serve, share and enjoy!

Smoked Beef Birria

Servings:4

Cooking Time: 240 Minutes

Ingredients:

- 8 lbs (3.6 kg) beef short ribs
- 8 guajillo chiles
- 5 ancho chiles
- 10 garlic cloves
- ½ oz (14 g) ginger
- 2 medium onions
- 2 cups (480 ml) water
- 2 tsp (10 ml) freshly ground black pepper
- ½ tsp (3 ml) ground cloves
- ½ tsp (3 ml) oregano
- 8 sprigs thyme
- ½ tsp (3 ml) ground cinnamon
- 4 bay leaves
- 3 tsp (15 ml) salt
- 4 tbsp (60 ml) vinegar

Directions:

1. Preheat the grill to 350°F using direct heat with a cast iron grate installed.

2. Clean the short ribs and marinate in ½ of adobo mix for 2 to 3 hours. Add the short ribs to the grid and smoke for 4 hours. Move the beef ribs to a dutch oven and cover with the remaining adobo; move the dutch oven to the kamado grill and cook for an additional 4 hours.

3. Enjoy with minced onion, cilantro and limes accompanied with tortillas.

4. In a dutch oven, cook chiles, garlic, ginger and onions in a pot with water, until chiles are tender. Drain the water and process together with the rest of the adobo ingredients.

Asian Beef & Mushroom Tacos

Servings: 4
Cooking Time: 25 Minutes

Ingredients:

- 1/2 head of green cabbage
- 1lb (450g) flank or round steak, cut into very thin strips
- kosher salt and freshly ground black pepper
- 3 tbsp vegetable oil, divided
- 1lb (450g) white mushrooms, sliced
- 4oz (110g) shredded carrots, fresh or pickled
- 1/3 cup hoisin sauce, plus more for serving
- 8 x 6-in (15.25-cm) flour tortillas
- 1/4 cup chopped fresh cilantro

Directions:

1. Preheat the grill to 425°F (218°C) using direct heat with a standard grate installed and a cast iron skillet on the grate. Place cabbage on the grate (not in the skillet) cut side down, close the lid, and grill until beginning to soften and char, about 7 to 10 minutes. Remove cabbage from the grill and slice finely. Set aside.

2. Season beef well with salt and pepper. Add 2 tbsp oil to the hot skillet and heat until shimmering. Add beef and cook until the meat has browned on both sides, about 5 to 6 minutes, turning once. Transfer to a platter and set aside. Return the skillet to the grill.

3. Add the remaining 1 tbsp oil to the skillet and heat until shimmering. Add mushrooms and cook until they're tender and all the liquid has evaporated, about 5 minutes. Add carrots and sliced cabbage to the skillet and cook until beginning to soften, about 2 minutes, stirring once or twice. Add the hoisin sauce and beef, stir to coat, and cook for 1 minute more.

4. Remove the taco mixture from the grill. To serve, scoop an equal portion of the mixture into each tortilla and top with cilantro and more hoisin sauce (if desired).

Smoked Oxtail Stew

Servings:6
Cooking Time: 240 Minutes

Ingredients:

- 3.5 lbs Oxtails
- 4 stalks celery, medium chopped
- 2 onions, medium chopped
- 8 oz cremini mushrooms, halved
- 1 small butternut squash, medium chopped
- 4 carrots, medium chopped
- Olive oil, salt, pepper (to brown)
- 6 tsp all purpose flour
- 3 tsp Louisiana Hot Sauce
- 1 tbs Creole seasoning
- 1 tbs granulated garlic
- 1 tbs fresh garlic
- 3 tbs whole grain dijon mustard
- 4 cups beef stock
- 2 tbs soy sauce
- 3 tbs ketchup
- 3 sprigs rosemary
- 2 x 14 oz cans chopped tomatoes
- 2 tbs salt
- 2 tbs pepper
- Mesquite and cherry wood, soaked in water
- Deep roaster foil pain (about 12" x 10" x 4")

Directions:

1. Oil, salt, and pepper the oxtails; brown on the grill with the cooking grid only. Let oxtails rest after browning.

2. Preheat the grill to 350°F using direct heat with a cast iron grate installed.

3. Cut all vegetables. Mix stock, mustard, soy, ketchup, and tomatoes in separate bowl. Place all vegetables, herbs, tails, and flour in a bowl and toss. Place mixture in a deep roasting pan and add liquid. Place soaked wood on fire and smoke for 4 hours at 350°F. Halfway through, cover with foil and stop adding wood.

4. After 4 hours, check tails for tenderness.

5. Enjoy with your favorite starch addition rice, potatoes, or pasta.

Red Gold Spicy Burgers

Servings:4
Cooking Time: 12 Minutes

Ingredients:

- 1 pound lean ground beef
- 1 (14.5 ounce) can Red Gold Petite Diced Tomatoes with Green Chilies, drained very well
- Salt and black pepper to taste
- For an added kick add a slice of pepper jack cheese into the center of each patty.
- Serve on toasted bun
- Top with Red Gold Mama Selita's Jalapeno Ketchup or Chipotle Mayo
- Top with slices of spicy peppers

Directions:

1. Preheat the grill to 400°F using direct heat with a cast iron grate installed.

2. Combine the ground beef and Red Gold Petite Diced Tomatoes with Green Chilies in a bowl. Form into patties and season with salt and black pepper.

3. Place directly on the cooking grid and cook for 5-6 minutes per side to desired temperature (160°F for completely cooked burgers).

Seared Bison Filet

Servings:6

Cooking Time: 10 Minutes

Ingredients:

- 8 oz bison filet
- 1 tsp salt
- 1 tsp pepper

Directions:

1. Preheat the grill to 500°F using direct heat with a cast iron grate installed with grillspander platesetter Basket in place for raised direct cooking.

2. Bring the bison to room temperature and season with salt and pepper. Place the filet on the cooking grid and grill for 5 minutes per side. Remove from the kamado grill when the internal temperature reaches 125°F.

3. Let rest 5 minutes before slicing and serving.

Grilled Top Blade Steak

Servings:4
Cooking Time: 7 Minutes

Ingredients:

- 2 top-blade steaks (about 1½ pounds), 1 to 1¼-inches thick Kosher salt
- 2 thick slices artisan bread, crusts removed and torn into ragged 1½-inch pieces
- 2 tablespoons extra-virgin olive oil, divided
- 1 teaspoon sherry or red wine vinegar
- 5 ounces baby arugula (about 6 cups)
- 1 cup lightly packed fresh herb leaves, such as basil, parsley, dill, chives, chervil, tarragon, mint, or a combination
- Finishing salt, such as coarse sea salt or flake salt
- Freshly ground black pepper

Directions:

1. Pat the steaks dry with a paper towel and season liberally with the kosher salt. Toss the

bread with 1 tablespoon of the olive oil and set it aside.

2. Preheat the grill to 450°F using direct heat with a cast iron grate installed, scrape the grid clean, and oil it lightly. Cook the steaks on the hottest part of the grill until seared, 3 to 3½ minutes. Use tongs to flip them and sear the second side for another 3 to 3½ minutes for medium rare. (To cook the steaks medium or beyond, slide them over to the coolest part of the kamado grill and close the cover, then cook for 1 to 4 minutes more.)

3. Grill the reserved bread croutons while the steaks rest, turning them 2 to 3 times, until they are tinged with brown.

4. Transfer the steaks to a cutting board. While they rest, make the salad dressing by whisking the vinegar with the remaining 1 tablespoon olive oil in a small bowl. Put the arugula and herbs in a salad bowl and toss with the dressing. Slice the steak against the grain into ½-inch-thick slices and put 4 to 5 slices on each plate. Pile a portion of the salad on top of each serving and balance a few croutons on top. Drizzle any meat juices from the cutting board over it all and sprinkle to taste with the finishing salt and black pepper.

Bacon Cheeseburger Hotdogs

Servings:8

Cooking Time: 16 Minutes

Ingredients:

- 8 good-quality all-beef hot dogs
- 8 Cobblestone Bread Co.™ Spud Dogs
- drizzle of ketchup
- drizzle of mustard
- chopped fresh parsley
- cheeseburger mixture
- white cheddar cheese sauce

- 6 strips of bacon, diced
- 1 pound ground beef
- 1-14 ounce can diced tomatoes, drained
- 2 tablespoons ketchup
- 1 tablespoon yellow mustard
- 1 ½ cups grated sharp cheddar cheese, divided
- salt and black pepper
- 2 tablespoons unsalted butter
- 2 tablespoons all-purpose flour
- 1 ½ cups whole milk
- 1 ½ cup grated white cheddar cheese
- pinch of cayenne pepper
- salt and black pepper

Directions:

1. Preheat the grill to 425°F using direct heat with a cast iron grate installed, and add your hot dogs to the grill. Grill for about 2 minutes on each side or until charred and warm. Remove from heat.

2. Assemble your bacon cheeseburger hot dogs, by placing each hot dog on Cobblestone Bread Co.™ Spud Dog. Top with the cheeseburger mixture and spoon the cheese sauce on top. Drizzle with ketchup and yellow mustard. Sprinkle with fresh parsley and the reserved bacon. Enjoy!

3. In a large, nonstick skillet, add the bacon. Fry over medium-low heat until crispy. Transfer the bacon to a plate that has been lined with a paper towel and pour out most of the bacon grease from the skillet. Place it back on the stove, and increase the heat to medium. Add the beef to the pan and cook until brown and cooked through, about 8 minutes. Decrease the heat to low, and add most of the bacon (reserving about 2 tablespoons for garnish) diced tomatoes, ketchup, yellow mustard, cheddar cheese, and salt and black

pepper. Stir until the cheese has melted. Cover and keep warm.

4. In a small saucepan, melt the butter for the white cheddar cheese sauce over medium heat. Whisk in the flour and cook for about 1 minute or until golden. Continuing to whisk, add the milk. Cook for about 3-4 minutes or until just slightly thickened. Remove from heat and stir in the white cheddar cheese until melted. Season with a pinch of cayenne pepper and salt and black pepper to taste. Cover and keep warm until you are ready to serve.

Short Ribs & Polenta

Servings: 4
Cooking Time: 200 Minutes

Ingredients:
- 8 beef short ribs
- 6 slices bacon, diced
- 3 carrots, diced
- 2 cloves garlic, minced
- 1 onion, diced
- 4 cups beef broth
- 1/2 cup red wine
- 1/4 cup flour
- 1 Tablespoon tomato paste
- 1/2 tsp ground fennel
- 2 sprigs fresh thyme
- 2 sprigs fresh rosemary
- Salt and Pepper
- 4 cups water
- 4 cups milk
- 2 cups polenta
- 1/2 cup sour cream
- 1/2 cup parmesan cheese, grated
- 3 Tablespoons butter
- 2 tsp salt

Directions:

1. Season the short ribs with salt and pepper and lightly dredge in the flour.
2. Place the bacon in a cold dutch oven over medium heat on the stove top.
3. Remove the bacon when it becomes crispy and set aside.
4. Working in batches, brown the short ribs on all sides. Set aside.
5. Remove all but 2 Tablespoon of the fat.
6. Add carrots, onion, and garlic and cook until soft.
7. Add tomato paste and cook for 2 minutes.
8. Add red wine and scrape the bottom of the dutch oven for 1 minute.
9. Add back bacon and beef, stir in fennel, thyme, and rosemary.
10. When there is 40 minutes left, bring the water, butter, and milk for the polenta to a simmer in a large sauce pan.
11. Add the salt and polenta to the water mixture and whisk constantly for 3-4 minutes.
12. Simmer partially covered for 45 minutes, stirring every 10 minutes.
13. Add sour cream and parmesan to the polenta and stir. Keep the polenta covered until you are ready to serve.
14. Grilling:
15. Preheat the grill to 325°F using direct heat with a cast iron grate installed.
16. Cover the dutch oven and transfer to the grill.
17. Close the dome for 2 1/2 hours.
18. When the ribs have been in the grill for 2 1/2 hours, close all the vents and allow the dutch oven to sit inside the grill for another 20 minutes.
19. Remove the dutch oven from the grill, remove stems from the herbs, and skim any fat that has come to the surface.
20. Serve two short ribs on a bed of creamy polenta.

Ray's At Killer Creek's Short Ribs

Servings:6
Cooking Time: 300 Minutes

Ingredients:

- 4 6" English cut short ribs
- 4 tbsp kosher salt - divided
- 2 tbsp brown sugar
- 6 whole garlic cloves - divided
- 2 sprigs thyme
- 2 bay leaves
- 1 tbsp fresh ground black pepper
- 4 rosemary sprigs
- 4 thyme sprigs
- 1 large carrot - cut into 1" pieces
- 2 whole celery stalks - cut into 1" pieces
- ½ yellow onion - peeled and cut into quarters
- 1 cup BBQ sauce - use your favorite sweet & smoky sauce
- 4 cups beef stock

Directions:

1. For the wet brine, combine 2 tbsp kosher salt, 2 tbsp brown sugar, 2 garlic cloves, 2 sprigs thyme, 2 bay leaves and 1 cup of water in small saucepot. Bring to a boil and simmer till salt and sugar are dissolved poor hot mixture over 2qts of ice in a plastic container. Submerge the short ribs in the brine and leave covered for 24 hours in refrigerator.

2. One hour before the cook, remove short ribs from brine to a plate and return to refrigerator to dry uncovered.

3. Preheat the grill to 275°F using direct heat with a cast iron grate installed.

4. Season the ribs on all sides with remaining salt and pepper and arrange on grill with 1" space between them. Scatter rosemary and thyme sprigs on top of ribs.

5. Cook for 3 hours until meat is caramel brown in color and starts to shrink up the bone. After 3 hours, place vegetables, remaining garlic, BBQ sauce and beef stock in a dutch oven or aluminum pan along with the ribs. Cover and continue cooking for 2 more hours.

6. Remove the short ribs with bones from the dutch oven. Purée sauce with vegetables and return short ribs and sauce to the dutch oven.

7. Serve individual portions over creamy stone ground grits and grilled asparagus, top with remainder of sauce.

Steakhouse Meatballs With French Fries And Tzatziki Sauce

Servings:4
Cooking Time: 30 Minutes

Ingredients:

- 1 lb. ground beef, 92% lean 8% fat
- 1 tbsp Steakhouse Seasoning
- 2 tbsp fresh parsley, chopped
- ⅓ cup grated Parmesan cheese
- Olive oil
- 1½ cup whole fat plain Greek yogurt
- ¾ cup cucumber, grated
- 2 tbsp fresh dill, chopped
- 2 cloves garlic, finely minced
- 1 tbsp lemon juice
- ½ tsp kosher salt
- 2 tbsp olive oil
- 2 russet potatoes, skin on, cut into lengthwise strips
- 1 qt water
- 2 tbsp Sweet & Smoky Seasoning
- Salt to taste
- 2 tbsp olive oil

Directions:

1. Preheat the grill to 400°F using direct heat with a cast iron grate installed. Place the half-moon cast iron griddle with the flat side up on top of the grid.

2. For the meatballs, mix the ground beef, Steakhouse Seasoning, and Parmesan cheese until uniform. Roll into inch sized balls. Place meatballs on the plancha, and cook until the internal temperature is 140°F. Remove from the kamado grill and let rest.

3. To plate, put a dollop of tzatziki sauce on the plate, top with meatballs, add fries to the side, and garnish with the parsley. Enjoy!

4. For the tzatziki sauce, mix all the ingredients together until uniform and refrigerate until needed.

5. Soak potatoes in water for 30 minutes, and then pat to dry. Let them air dry for 5 to 10 minutes. Coat them in olive oil, a pinch or two of salt and the Sweet & Smoky Seasoning. Place them into the roasting pan, making sure the potatoes are all flat on the pan. Bake for 30 minutes or until the potatoes are golden brown.

Korean-style Beef Short Ribs

Servings: 8
Cooking Time: 12 Minutes

Ingredients:

- 3lb (1.4kg) flanken-style beef ribs, cut 1/4-in (.5-cm) thick
- for the marinade
- 1 medium ripe pear, peeled and diced
- 6 garlic cloves, roughly chopped
- 1 tbsp chili garlic sauce
- 1 tbsp minced fresh ginger
- 3 tbsp toasted sesame oil
- 6 tbsp sugar

- 2 tbsp rice vinegar
- 3 scallions, thinly sliced
- kimchi (optional), to serve

Directions:

1. To make the marinade, in a food processor, combine pear, garlic, chili garlic sauce, ginger, sesame oil, sugar, and rice vinegar. Pulse until smooth, and stir in the scallions. Reserve 1/3 cup marinade.

2. Place ribs in a large resealable plastic bag and pour the remaining marinade over top. Squeeze out any excess air and refrigerate for 6 to 24 hours, turning once or twice.

3. Preheat the grill to 400°F (204°C) using direct heat with a cast iron grate installed. Place ribs on the grate, close the lid, and cook until browned, about 6 to 12 minutes, turning 2 to 3 times.

4. On the stovetop in a small saucepan over medium heat, warm the reserved marinade. Remove ribs from the grill, place on a large serving platter, and spoon the warmed marinade over top. Serve immediately with kimchi (if using).

Beef Asparagus Stir Fry

Servings:4
Cooking Time: 10 Minutes

Ingredients:

- 1 lb. boneless beef short rib, sliced thin
- ½ cup soy sauce
- ¼ cup oyster sauce
- 2 tsp corn starch
- 1 tbsp rice wine vinegar
- 3 cloves garlic, minced
- 2 tbsp ginger, minced
- 2 tbsp canola oil
- 1 bunch of asparagus, cut in to 1" segments

- Chopped green onion for garnish

Directions:

1. One day before the cook mix together the soy sauce, oyster sauce, corn starch, rice wine vinegar, garlic and ginger. Marinate the beef overnight in the mixture.

2. Preheat the grill to 500°F using direct heat with a cast iron grate installed(close the bottom vent before adding the wok).

3. Heat the canola oil in the wok. Add the marinated beef and stir fry. Once the sauce reduces and becomes a nice glaze, add the asparagus and stir fry until bright green.

4. Serve over rice and garnish with chopped green onion.

Smoked Beef Brisket

Servings: 38

Cooking Time: 900 Minutes

Ingredients:

- 1¼ cups sugar
- 2⁄3 cup ground black pepper
- 2⁄3 cup seasoned salt
- 2⁄3 cup kosher salt
- 2½ tbsp ground cayenne pepper
- 15lb (6.8kg) whole beef brisket, trimmed of fat
- pickle slices (optional), to serve
- BBQ sauce (optional), to serve
- to smoke
- post oak, hickory, or mesquite wood chunks

Directions:

1. In a medium bowl, combine sugar, pepper, seasoned salt, kosher salt, and cayenne. Rub brisket with the seasoning mixture. Wrap tightly with plastic wrap and refrigerate for 24 hours.

2. Preheat the grill to 225°F (107°C). Once hot, add the wood chunks, install the heat deflector, place a drip pan on top, and install a standard grate. Remove brisket from the fridge and allow to come to room temperature.

3. Place the brisket fat side up on the grate, close the lid, and smoke until the internal temperature reaches 160°F (71°C), about 5 to 7 hours. Remove brisket from the grill, wrap heavily in aluminum foil, and return to the grill to continue to cook until the internal temperature reaches 185°F (85°C), about 8 hours. (Check the texture of the meat for doneness throughout the cooking process). The total cook time is about 15 hours, or 1 hour per pound (approximately 2 hours per kilogram).

4. Transfer brisket to a serving platter and let rest for 20 minutes. Slice or shred the meat, and serve with pickle slices and BBQ sauce (if desired).

Round Roast Cheesesteaks With Pepper Jack Cheese Sauce

Servings: 8

Cooking Time: 40 Minutes

Ingredients:

- 1 (2-3 lb) Round Roast
- 2 Tablespoons olive oil
- 6 crusty hoagie rolls
- 1 large onion, sliced
- 1/4 cup Garlic Lovers' Rub
- 2 cups whole milk
- 1 cup Pepper Jack cheese
- 2 Tablespoons butter
- 2 Tablespoons flour
- 1/2 tsp salt
- 1/4 tsp sriracha

Directions:

1. Bring round roast to room temperature.

2. Spread liberally with Garlic Lover's' Rub.

3. In a medium skillet, heat olive oil and cook onion slowly until caramelized, about 20 minutes.

4. Meanwhile, in a small sauce pan, melt butter and stir in flour. Cook an additional 1 minute.

5. Slowly add milk, whisking continually until thickened.

6. Remove the sauce from the heat, add salt, sriracha, and cheese, and stir to combine.

7. Grilling:

8. Preheat the grill to 475°F using direct heat with a cast iron grate installed.

9. Place the roast on the grid and close the dome for 10 minutes.

10. Reduce the heat inside the grill to 325°F and continue to cook for 25-30 minutes or until the internal temperature reaches 130°F.

11. Remove from the grill and set aside to rest while cooking the onions and making the cheese sauce.

12. Thinly slice the beef, adding several slices to a hoagie roll. Top with onion and cheese sauce and serve.

London Bridge London Broil

Servings: 4
Cooking Time: 10 Minutes

Ingredients:
- 1 (1 1/2 -2 pound) London Broil
- 1/2 tsp salt
- 1/4 tsp pepper
- 4 Tablespoons Herb Compound Butter

Directions:

1. Season both sides with salt and pepper.

2. Grilling:

3. Preheat the grill to 500°F using direct heat with a cast iron grate installed.

4. Place London Broil on the grid and close the dome for 3 minutes.

5. Flip the steak over and cook an additional 2 minutes.

6. Close all of the vents and let the steak sit for 5 minutes or until the internal temperature reaches 130°F.

7. Remove the steak and immediately top with dots of Herb Compound Butter.

8. Allow it to rest for 10 minutes before slicing thinly across the grain.

Pulled Lamb Nachos

Servings:4
Cooking Time: 5 Minutes

Ingredients:
- 1 lamb shoulder, bone in
- 2/3 cup apple juice, hot
- 2 tbsp BBQ spice (your favorite)
- 3/4 lb. corn chips, preferably artisanal
- 1 cup of shredded mozzarella
- 1 cup of shredded cheddar cheese
- 10 cherry tomatoes, sliced
- 2 tbsp sliced Kalamata olives
- 1 jalapeno pepper, chopped
- 3 tbsp minced green onions
- ¼ cup chopped fresh coriander, as garnish
- 1/2 cup sour cream, to serve
- 1/2 cup salsa, to serve

Directions:

1. Preheat the grill to 250°F using direct heat with a cast iron grate installed.

2. Smoke the lamb shoulder for 4-5 hours until internal temperature reaches 195°F. Remove from the grill, cover with foil and rest for at least 30 minutes. Once cooled, pull the meat.

3. Mix together the apple juice and BBQ sauce. Cover the meat with the mixture.

4. Preheat the grill to 350°F using direct heat with a cast iron grate installed.

5. Place the tortilla chips on a round pan and top with cheese, pulled lamb, tomatoes, olives, and jalapeños. Put the pan on back on the kamado grill and cook for 5 minutes, or until cheese is fully melted.

6. Remove from the kamado grill and top with green onions and coriander. Serve with sour cream and salsa.

Ultimate Bacon Jam Burger

Servings:4
Cooking Time: 75 Minutes

Ingredients:

- 1 ½ pounds ground beef 80/20 chuck roast
- 1 teaspoon kosher salt
- ½ teaspoon fresh ground black pepper
- 4 Cobblestone Bread Co.™ Corn Dusted Kaiser Rolls
- 1 tablespoon grapeseed or canola oil
- 4 tablespoons goat cheese, softened
- 8 slices tomato
- 1 cup arugula
- Sundried tomato bacon jam
- 10 sundried tomatoes
- 10 ounces bacon, cut into 1" sections
- 2 yellow onions, peeled and sliced
- ½ cup water
- ⅓ cup light brown sugar
- 3 tablespoons apple cider vinegar
- ½ teaspoon black pepper

Directions:

1. Divide the ground meat into four round patties and place in the refrigerator 2 hours before cooking. Preheat the grill to 500°F using direct heat with a cast iron grate installed. Season burgers equally with salt and pepper, place on the kamado grill and close the dome. Cook for 4 minutes, flip, and cook for another 4 minutes with dome closed or until the internal temperature reaches 145-150°F for medium-rare. Transfer to a plate and allow to rest for 5 to 10 minutes.

2. While the burgers are resting, brush oil on burger buns and grill for 1 minute until the buns are lightly toasted. To assemble, place a burger patty on the bottom bun and top with goat cheese, then 2 tomato slices, and arugula. Spread a spoonful of bacon jam on the top bun and place on top of the arugula. Serve immediately.

3. Soak sundried tomatoes in hot water for 10 minutes. Drain and slice into thin strips. In a large heavy-bottomed pot over medium-high heat, cook bacon until cooked through and crisp. Add onions and sauté until tender, about 5 minutes. Add tomatoes, water, brown sugar, vinegar, and black pepper and bring to a boil. Reduce heat to a low simmer and simmer for 45 to 60 minutes until thickened and the water has completely reduced. Remove from heat and allow to cool for 10 minutes then place in a blender or food processor and puree. Can be made up to a week in advance and stored in the refrigerator.

Ny Strip Steaks

Servings:4
Cooking Time: 13 Minutes

Ingredients:

- 4 NY Strip steaks, seasoned with 4 tbsp Dizzy Gourmet Cosmic Cow Seasoning™
- 1 Tablespoon unsalted butter
- ¼ cup mushrooms, cut into bite size pieces
- ¼ cup chopped leeks
- 1 clove garlic, minced
- ½ cup whiskey

- 2 cups heavy cream
- ⅛ teaspoon cayenne pepper
- Salt and pepper

Directions:

1. Preheat the grill to 650°F using direct heat with a cast iron grate installed.

2. Grill steaks to desired internal temperature. 2 ½ minutes, then flip. 2 ½ minutes, then flip. Cook additional 3 minutes.

3. Set aside and keep warm.

4. Reduce heat to 350°F. Set a cast iron skillet or dutch oven on the grid and let it heat up for a few minutes. Add the butter and cook it until lightly brown, then add the mushrooms and cook until tender. Stir in leeks and garlic.

5. Slowly add the whiskey, it will ignite, so seriously, add it slowly! Once the whiskey burns off, stir and close the lid of the grill. Cook until the whiskey reduces by two-thirds. Add the cream, and stir frequently for 3 to 4 minutes. Add a little cayenne pepper and then add salt and pepper if you'd like.

6. Put the steaks on the grid and close the lid. Grill for about 4 minutes for medium-rare, turning once. Move the steaks to plates. Pour the sauce over the steaks and serve.

Pastrami Beef Short Ribs

Servings:8
Cooking Time: 120 Minutes

Ingredients:

- 1 Whole Snake River Farms Beef Plate Short Rib
- Corning Brine
- Pastrami Rub
- 1 gallon water
- 1½ cups Kosher salt
- ¾ cups granulated sugar
- ¾ cups brown sugar
- 1 Tbsp + 2 tsp Tinted Cure Mix #1 (Pink Salt)
- 4 bay leaves, crushed
- 1 Tbsp juniper berries, crushed
- 10 cloves, whole
- 1 Tbsp black peppercorns, crushed
- 1 Tbsp coriander seeds, crushed
- 1 Tbsp mustard seeds
- 5 garlic cloves, crushed
- ¼ cup honey
- 1 cup black peppercorns, coarsely ground
- ½ cup coriander seeds, coarsely ground
- ½ cup onion powder
- ½ cup granulated garlic powder
- ¼ cup juniper berries, ground

Directions:

1. Combine all of the brine ingredients in a large pot and bring to a simmer. Simmer for 15 minutes, then cool and store overnight in the refrigerator. Place the whole short rib in a 2 gallon zipper bag. Then pour the cold brine in the bag. The bag should hold the full gallon of brine. Let the rib brine for a minimum of 48 hours. Flip the bag over each day.

2. Grind the peppercorns and coriander seeds in a mortar and pestle or a coffee grinder for the best results. Start with a full cup of each before you grind them. After grinding, combine the peppercorns and coriander seeds with the onion powder, garlic powder and the ground Juniper berries.

3. Remove the short rib from the brine. Pat dry with a paper towel. Liberally coat the rib with the pastrami rub. Do not be afraid to go heavy with this rub!

4. Preheat the grill to 275°F using direct heat with a cast iron grate installed.

5. Place the short ribs meat side up in the smoker. Smoke the ribs for two hours at 275°F. Next, reduce the temperature to 250°F. Smoke until the rib reaches an internal temperature of 185°F.

6. At this stage, wrap ribs in butcher's paper, or place in a large paper grocery bag. Once wrapped, place back in the smoker until the ribs reach an internal temperature of 203°F. Remove from the smoker and allow the rib to rest in the paper for 20-25 minutes before serving.

Smoked Bourbon Chili

Servings:8
Cooking Time: 245 Minutes

Ingredients:
- 4 tbsp olive oil, separated
- 2 lbs. ground sirloin
- 1 lb. Italian sausage
- 2 onions, diced
- 1 green bell pepper, seeded and diced
- 1 red bell pepper, seeded and diced
- 2 jalapeno chiles, seeded and finely chopped
- 2 serrano chiles, seeded and finely chopped
- 4 cloves of garlic, minced
- 1 28 oz can crushed tomatoes, with liquid
- 1 10 oz can rotel tomatoes
- 2 tbsp tomato paste
- 1 15 oz can kidney beans, drained
- 1 15 oz can chili beans
- 1 15 oz can white beans, drained
- 3 tbsp chili powder
- 1 tbsp ancho chile powder
- 1 tbsp ground cumin
- 1 tsp cocoa powder
- 1 tbsp brown sugar
- 1 tsp ground cinnamon
- 1 tsp dried oregano

- 3 tbsp Ancho Chili & Coffee seasoning
- 2 Tb Tabasco Sauce
- 1 cup red wine
- 2 oz bourbon
- 2 cups beef broth
- 2 bay leaves
- 2 dried ancho chili peppers to float on top

Directions:
1. Preheat the grill to 350°F using direct heat with a cast iron grate installed.
2. Place cast iron dutch oven on the kamado grill and add olive oil. Let it heat up for a few minutes. Add the ground sirloin and sausage and stir to break the meat up into small pieces. Cook for about 1 hour, stirring every 10-15 minutes. Remove dutch oven from the grill, drain the meat, and set aside.
3. Return the dutch oven to the grill, add 2 more tbsp of olive oil and sauté onions, green and red peppers, jalapeños and serrano peppers for about 10 minutes. Add garlic and continue cooking for 2-3 minutes. Add remaining ingredients and the meat. Cook, uncovered, for about 2-3 hours
4. Remove bay leaves and dried chiles before serving.

Stir-fry Szechuan Beef

Servings:4
Cooking Time: 7 Minutes

Ingredients:
- 1 pound Certified Angus Beef flank steak, cut against grain into ¼-inch thick strips
- 4 tbsp soy sauce, divided
- 4 tbsp rice wine (Shaoxing), divided
- 1 tbsp cornstarch
- 1 tbsp rice wine vinegar
- 2 tbsp canola oil

- 3 cloves garlic, minced
- 2 teaspoons Szechuan peppercorns, crushed (or 1-teaspoon of each, chili flake and black pepper)
- 2 tablespoons oyster sauce (or hoisin sauce)
- 10 small red chilies, halved and seeded
- 4 scallions, cut into 2-inch segments

Directions:

1. Combine 2 tablespoons soy sauce, 2 tablespoons rice wine, cornstarch and rice wine vinegar in a mixing bowl; whisk together. Add sliced flank steak and marinate for 30 minutes to 1 hour.

2. Preheat the grill to 500°F using direct heat with a cast iron grate installed.

3. Remove steak strips from marinade, pat dry and discard marinade. Heat the oil in a Carbon Steel Wok; add beef strips and stir constantly for 2-3 minutes to cook evenly.

4. Stir in garlic and Szechuan peppercorns and stir-fry another minute. Reduce heat to medium, add remaining soy sauce, rice wine, oyster sauce, chilies and scallions.

5. Sear 3-4 minutes, stirring often until sauce thickens and glazes meat. Enjoy!

Ray's Herb Butter Prime Rib

Servings:6
Cooking Time: 120 Minutes

Ingredients:

- 5 pound boneless ribeye roast
- Kosher salt
- Black pepper, coarse ground
- 2 sticks of butter, at room temperature
- 4 cloves garlic, crushed
- ¼ cup chopped fresh thyme leaves
- ¼ cup chopped fresh tarragon leaves
- ¼ cup chopped fresh parsley

- Au Jus and Horseradish Sauce for serving

Directions:

1. Preheat the grill to 325°F using direct heat with a cast iron grate installed. Season the roast liberally with the salt and pepper. In a medium bowl, mix together the butter, garlic, and herbs. Spread the herb butter evenly all over the roast. Place roast on the cooking grid. Cook it until it reaches an internal temperature of 125°F in the center for medium rare. This will take about 1½ to 2 hours. Remove to a platter and tent loosely with foil. Let rest for 15 minutes. Slice thick for prime rib type slabs or thin for a roast beef presentation.

Reverse-sear Ribeye

Servings: 4
Cooking Time: 80 Minutes

Ingredients:

- 2lb (1kg) ribeye steak
- 1 tbsp vegetable oil
- kosher salt and freshly ground black pepper
- for the sauce
- 3 red bell peppers, left whole
- ½ bunch of scallions, trimmed
- ⅓ cup whole almonds
- 3 large garlic cloves
- ½ tsp crushed red pepper flakes
- 2 tbsp lemon juice
- ½ tsp kosher salt
- ¼ cup extra virgin olive oil
- to smoke
- pecan or bourbon barrel wood chunks

Directions:

1. Preheat the grill to 225°F (107°C). Once hot, add the wood chunks and install the heat deflector and a standard grate with a cast iron skillet on the grate.

2. In the hot skillet, place almonds and toast until golden brown, about 10 to 15 minutes, stirring occasionally. Remove the skillet from the grill and set aside.

3. Rub steak with oil, season with salt and pepper to taste, and place on the grate. Smoke until the internal temperature reaches 115°F (46°C), about 30 minutes per pound (approximately 1 hour per kilogram). Transfer to a platter and set aside.

4. Remove the heat deflector, replace the standard grate with a cast iron grate, and open the top and bottom vents to raise the grill temperature to 500°F (260°C) using direct heat. Place peppers and scallions on the grate, and grill until beginning to soften and char, about 3 minutes per side, turning once. Remove from the grill, seed and roughly chop the peppers, and roughly chop the scallions.

5. To make the sauce, in a food processor, combine almonds, garlic, and red pepper flakes, and pulse until finely ground. Add peppers, scallions, lemon juice, and salt, and purée, adding oil in a slow stream. Season with black pepper to taste.

6. Place steak on the grate and sear until steak reaches your desired level of doneness, about 2 to 3 minutes per side for medium rare. Transfer to a cutting board and thinly slice. Top with the romesco sauce, and serve immediately.

Taco Soup

Servings: 8
Cooking Time: 60 Minutes

Ingredients:
- 1 lb ground beef
- 4 cups chicken broth
- 1/2 cup chopped onion
- 1 Tablespoon garlic, minced
- 1 Tablespoon chili powder
- 1 Tablespoon smoked paprika
- 1 tsp ground cumin
- 2 cans pinto beans, rinsed and drained
- 1 can black beans, rinsed and drained
- 1 can corn, drained
- Salt & Pepper

Directions:
1. Place ingredients in a cold dutch oven and stir.
2. Grilling:
3. Preheat the grill to 350°F using direct heat with a cast iron grate installed.
4. Place the dutch oven on the grid of the grill and lower the dome for 1 hour.
5. Soup is done when the ground beef is cooked through.
6. Serve with shredded cheese, cut up avocado, shredded cabbage and tortilla chips.

Grilled Buffalo Steaks

Servings:4
Cooking Time: 8 Minutes

Ingredients:
- Half moon cast iron griddle
- Honey Date Butter
- 1/4 cup (60 mL) butter, softened
- 1 shallot, minced
- 1/2 cup (125 mL) dried pitted honey dates (approx. 6), coarsely chopped 1 tbsp (15 mL) honey
- 1 tsp (5 mL) chopped fresh sage
- Splash of cognac
- Pinch of nutmeg
- Kosher salt and freshly ground black pepper to taste

- 4 buffalo strip loin steaks (5 to 6 oz/140 to 170 g each), cut 1½ inches (4 cm) thick 2 tsp (10 mL) Steak Spice (page 169)
- Drizzle of honey
- ½ cup (125 mL) sliced almonds

Directions:

1. To prepare the Honey Date Butter, mix the softened butter with the shallot pieces, dates, honey and sage in a bowl. Add a splash of cognac and season to taste with a pinch of nutmeg, kosher salt and black pepper. Mix and set aside at room temperature.

2. Season buffalo steaks with the Steak Spice, pressing the seasoning into the meat. Preheat the grill to 600°F using direct heat with a cast iron grate installed.

3. Toast the sliced almonds over the hot fire in half moon cast iron griddle, flipping the almonds to keep them from sticking and burning. Remove once toasted and set aside, keeping warm.

4. Grill steaks directly over the fire with the dome open for 3–4 minutes per side for rare to medium-rare doneness. After the flip, spoon a small amount of the Honey Date Butter over the steaks and brush it into the meat. Remove buffalo steaks from kamado grill and let rest for 5 minutes, tented loosely with a sheet of aluminum foil.

5. Slice the steaks on the bias and serve with a little extra dollop of Honey Date Butter. Garnish with toasted sliced almonds and a drizzle of honey.

Pimento Cheese Burger With Bacon Jam

Servings:4
Cooking Time: 12 Minutes

Ingredients:

- 4 Nature's Own 100% Whole Wheat Buns
- 4 seasoned burger patties
- 1 cup prepared pimento cheese spread
- 1-2 sliced plum tomatoes
- 2 cups romaine lettuce
- ½ cup sweet onion slices
- 1 cup crumbled bacon pieces
- 3 tablespoons maple syrup
- 1 tablespoon balsamic vinegar glaze

Directions:

1. In a food processor, mix the bacon, maple syrup and balsamic glaze until it is fully incorporated to make the bacon jam. It will look like a textured spread, then set aside.

2. Preheat the grill to 400°F using direct heat with a cast iron grate installed.

3. Cook burgers 5-6 minutes per side to desired temperature.

4. Layer bun with burger, pimento cheese, lettuce, onion, tomato and bacon jam. Top burger with bun top and serve.

Herbed-up Prime Rib

Servings:8
Cooking Time: 150 Minutes

Ingredients:

- 1 (4-pound) bone-in standing rib roast
- Kosher salt and black pepper
- 4 tablespoons salted butter, at room temperature
- 1 tablespoon finely chopped fresh basil
- 1 tablespoon finely chopped fresh tarragon
- 1 tablespoon finely chopped fresh rosemary

Directions:

1. One hour before you plan to cook, take the roast out of the refrigerator. Preheat the grill to 350°F using direct heat with a cast iron grate

installed. Season the roast on all sides with salt and pepper. In a small bowl, combine the butter, basil, tarragon and rosemary and mix well. Spread the herb butter all over the roast, applying the heaviest layer to the fat cap.

2. Place the roast, fat side up, on the kamado grill cooking grid and cook for about 2 hours, or until it reaches an internal temperature deep in the center of 125°F for medium-rare.

3. Transfer the roast to a platter, tent loosely with foil and let rest for at least 20 minutes or up to 30 minutes. Cut the meat away from the bones and slice the roast thickly or thinly against the grain as desired. Separate the leftover beef rib bones and serve them along with the meat.

Korean Short Ribs

Servings: 4
Cooking Time: 6 Minutes

Ingredients:
- 12 flanken style beef short ribs (about 4 lbs)
- 1 recipe Korean Barbecue Marinade

Directions:
1. Pour the marinade in a large zip top bag. Add short ribs. Seal and let sit in the fridge at least 4 hours, preferably overnight.
2. Remove short ribs from the oven before preheating the grill.
3. Grilling:
4. Preheat the grill to 500°F using direct heat with a cast iron grate installed.
5. Place the ribs directly on the grid and close the dome for 3 minutes.
6. Turn the ribs and cook an additional 2 minutes.
7. Remove the ribs, close all vents to extinguish the fire, and serve.

BURGERS

Breakfast Burger

Servings: 4

Cooking Time: 13 Minutes

Ingredients:

- 1 1/2 lb ground beef
- 1/2 lb ground pork breakfast sausage
- 2 Tablespoon butter
- 8 strips bacon
- 4 slices sharp cheddar cheese
- 4 Brioche buns
- 4 eggs
- 4 thick slices tomato

Directions:

1. In a medium bowl, mix ground beef and sausage until just combined.

2. Form into 4 patties and refrigerate while the grill heats.

3. Melt butter in a large skillet and fry the eggs for 2 minutes on each side.

4. Grilling:

5. Preheat the grill to 400°F using direct heat with a cast iron grate installed.

6. Place bacon on a small cookie sheet and place on the grid in the grill. Cook until crispy.

7. Place the patties on the grid and close the dome for 3 minutes.

8. Flip the burgers and replace the dome for an additional 3 minutes.

9. Close all of the vents and allow the burgers to sit for an additional 5 minutes. The internal temperature of the burger should be 150°F.

10. Place cheese on top of the burgers and cover for 1 more minute.

11. Assemble the burgers by placing a burger on the bottom bun, topping with bacon, tomato, and a fried egg.

Classic American Burger

Servings: 4

Cooking Time: 12 Minutes

Ingredients:

- 2 lbs ground beef
- 1/2 tsp salt
- 1/4 tsp pepper
- 4 slices American cheese
- 4 hamburger buns
- Green Leaf Lettuce
- Sliced Tomato
- Ketchup
- Mustard
- Sliced Pickle

Directions:

1. Form ground beef into four patties and season both sides with salt and pepper.

2. Grilling:

3. Preheat the grill to 500°F using direct heat with a cast iron grate installed.

4. Place burgers on the grid and close the dome for 3 minutes.

5. Flip burgers and close the dome for 2 more minutes.

6. Close all of the vents and allow the burgers to sit for 5 minutes.

7. Top each burger with a slice of cheese and close the dome for 1 more minute.

8. Build burgers with lettuce, tomato, pickle, mustard, and ketchup.

Oahu Burger

Servings: 4
Cooking Time: 12 Minutes

Ingredients:
- 2 lbs ground beef
- 1/4 cup thickened Teriyaki Marinade
- 1/4 cup mayonnaise
- 1/2 tsp sambal or sriracha
- 4 slices fresh pineapple, cored
- 4 slices tomato
- 4 slices butter lettuce
- 4 Hawaiian hamburger buns

Directions:
1. Form ground beef into four patties and season both sides with salt and pepper.
2. In a small bowl, mix mayonnaise with hot chile sauce and spread on buns.
3. Top each bun with a burger, slice of pineapple, lettuce and tomato.
4. Grilling:
5. Preheat the grill to 500°F using direct heat with a cast iron grate installed.
6. Place burgers on the grid and close the dome for 3 minutes.
7. Flip burgers, baste with Teriyaki Marinade, and place the pineapple slices on the grid. Close the dome for 2 more minutes.
8. Flip the burgers again and baste with remaining Teriyaki Marinade. Close the dome.
9. Close all of the vents and allow the burgers to sit for 5 minutes.

Quesadilla Burger

Servings: 4
Cooking Time: 12 Minutes

Ingredients:
- 2 lbs ground beef
- 2 Tablespoons Adobo Rub
- 1 cup shredded cheddar cheese
- 4 large flour tortillas
- Sour Cream
- Guacamole
- Salsa

Directions:
1. Form ground beef into four patties and season both sides with Adobo Rub.
2. Serve each burger with sour cream, guacamole, and salsa.
3. Grilling:
4. Preheat the grill to 500°F using direct heat with a cast iron grate installed.
5. Place burgers on the grid and close the dome for 3 minutes.
6. Flip burgers and close the dome for 2 more minutes.
7. Close all of the vents and allow the burgers to sit for 5 minutes.
8. Remove burgers and place flour tortillas on the grid.
9. Top each tortilla with shredded cheese and close the dome for 1 minute until the cheese melts.
10. Place a hamburger in the center of each tortilla and begin folding the tortilla around the burger like an envelope.

The Crowned Jewels Burger

Servings: 4
Cooking Time: 12 Minutes

Ingredients:
- 2 lbs ground beef
- 1/2 tsp salt
- 1/4 tsp pepper
- 1 lb thinly sliced pastrami
- 1 cup shredded Romaine lettuce

- 1/4 cup mayonnaise
- 2 Tablespoons ketchup
- 1/8 tsp onion powder
- 4 slices Sharp Cheddar cheese
- 4 hamburger buns
- 1 tomato, sliced

Directions:

1. Form ground beef into four patties and season both sides with salt and pepper.

2. Meanwhile, mix together mayonnaise, ketchup, and onion powder. Smear on each bun.

3. Place each pastrami and cheese covered burger on the prepared buns and top with shredded lettuce and tomato.

4. Grilling:

5. Preheat the grill to 500°F using direct heat with a cast iron grate installed.

6. Place burgers on the grid and close the dome for 3 minutes.

7. Flip burgers and close the dome for 2 more minutes.

8. Close all of the vents and allow the burgers to sit for 5 minutes.

9. Top each burger with 1/4 of the pastrami and a slice of cheese and close the dome for 1 more minute.

"the Masterpiece"

Servings: 4

Cooking Time: 12 Minutes

Ingredients:
- 2 lbs ground beef
- 6 ounces sliced mushrooms
- 4 Tablespoons shredded smoked Gouda
- 2 Tablespoons butter
- 2 Tablespoons olive oil
- 2 Tablespoons Dijon mustard
- 1/2 tsp salt

- 1/4 tsp pepper
- 8 slices bacon, cooked and crumbled
- 4 slices Swiss cheese
- 4 brioche buns
- 1 small onion, sliced

Directions:

1. Heat a skillet over medium heat and add 1 Tablespoon butter and 1 Tablespoon olive oil.

2. Place mushrooms in the pan and DO NOT MOVE THEM. Saute for 5-7 minutes or until the mushrooms are browned. Remove from the pan and set aside.

3. In the same skillet, heat remaining butter and olive oil and add onions. Saute over medium heat until they become translucent and begin to brown, about 10 minutes. Remove from the heat and set aside to cool.

4. Mix onion, mushrooms, and crumbled bacon.

5. Grilling:

6. Preheat the grill to 425°F using direct heat with a cast iron grate installed.

7. Form ground beef into eight patties and season both sides with salt and pepper.

8. Place a generous spoonful of the mushroom and onion mixture in the center of four patties and top with smoked Gouda.

9. Top with additional patty and press sides to seal the mixture inside.

10. Place burgers on the grid and close the dome for 5 minutes.

11. Flip burgers and close the dome for 3 more minutes.

12. Close all of the vents and allow the burgers to sit for 5 minutes.

13. Top each burger with a slice of Swiss cheese and close the dome for 1 more minute.

14. Spread buns with mustard, top with burgers and bun tops.

PORK

Reuben Riffel's Yellow Bellied Pork

Servings:4

Cooking Time: 130 Minutes

Ingredients:

- 1/2 pork belly, deboned, fat scored finely
- 3 tbsp (45 ml) coarse salt
- 4 sprigs fresh thyme
- 1 1/2 cups (360 ml) curry sauce
- 8 dried apricots
- 1 cup (240 ml) water
- 1 cup (240 ml) sugar
- 2 star anise
- 2 tsp (10 ml) ground cinnamon
- 1 tbsp (15 ml) vegetable oil
- 2 medium onions, chopped
- 1/2 cup (120 ml) white wine vinegar
- 1 tsp (5 ml) garlic, chopped
- 1 tsp (5 ml) ginger, chopped
- 2 tbsp (30 ml) curry powder
- 2 tbsp (30 ml) garam masala
- 1 tbsp (15 ml) turmeric
- 1 tbsp (15 ml) paprika
- 3 allspice/pimentos
- 2 bay leaves
- 1 cup (240 ml) whole peeled tomatoes
- 1 cup (240 ml) water
- 1 cup (240 ml) chicken stock
- 1/2 cup (120 ml) sugar
- 1 tsp (5 ml) salt
- 1 tsp (5 ml) ground black pepper

Directions:

1. Rub the pork belly evenly with salt, focusing on the fatty part. Rub in the thyme evenly. Let cure for 30 minutes.

2. Preheat the grill to 325°F using direct heat with a cast iron grate installed. Place a drip pan on the platesetter and then add the stainless steel grid.

3. Dust the excess salt off the pork belly and add to the cooking grid, fatty side up. Cook for one hour and 40 minutes; flipping the meat over halfway through. Remove from the heat and let rest for 10 minutes before slicing. Serve drizzled with warm curry sauce and poached apricots.

4. Bring all the ingredients except the apricots to a boil. Turn down to a simmer, add the apricots and poach for two to three minutes. Remove from the heat and strain.

5. Set the kamado grill for direct cooking (without the platesetter) at 350°F.

6. Add the oil to a Stir-Fry & Paella Pan and cook the onions and spices until soft and fragrant. Deglaze the onion mixture with white wine vinegar and reduce the kamado grill temperature to 300°F.

7. Add the rest of the ingredients and cook for 20 to 30 minutes, or until the sauce has thickened to a thick gravy consistency. Blend until smooth and strain.

Smoked Pork Loin Sandwich

Servings:4

Cooking Time: 5 Minutes

Ingredients:

- 7 lb (3 kg) center cut pork loin
- Dizzy Gourmet Down and DizzyTM Seasoning

- Hamburger Buns
- Barbecue Sauce
- 2 Spanish onions, sliced into thin rings
- 2 cups (480 ml) buttermilk
- 2 cups (480 ml) all purpose flour
- 1 tsp (5 ml) kosher salt
- 1 tbsp (15 ml) ground black pepper
- 1/2 tsp (3 ml) cayenne pepper
- Vegetable oil for cooking the onions

Directions:

1. Preheat the grill to 250°F using direct heat with a cast iron grate installed.

2. Season pork loin on all sides and let rest 30 minutes while the kamado grill temperature stabilizes. Place the pork loin in a V-Rack and place on the cooking rid; cook until the internal temperature reaches 160°F, then remove to a pan and refrigerate. Once the pork loin is cool, slice the pork thin, almost like deli ham or turkey thickness.

3. Thinly slice the Spanish onions an soak them in buttermilk for at least one hour.

4. Set the kamado grill for direct cooking (without the platesetter) at 400°F.

5. Remove onions from buttermilk bath and shake off excess buttermilk. Prepare seasoned flour by mixing all purpose flour, kosher salt, black pepper and cayenne pepper. Toss the slices and soaked onions in the season flour, covering thoroughly.

6. Add a dutch oven to the cooking grid and add about 1/2 inch of oil to preheat. Add the seasoned onions and cook until golden brown; set aside.

7. Carefully drain the oil from the dutch oven, return to the grid and sauté slices of the pork loin in the barbecue sauce until hot, approximately 3-5 minutes.

8. Toast the hamburger buns, add sliced pork loin, top with fried onion strings.

Bacon Roses

Servings:12
Cooking Time: 10 Minutes

Ingredients:
- Bouquet of rose stems or wooden skewers
- 1 pack of bacon
- 40 toothpicks
- Sweet and Smoky Seasoning

Directions:

1. Preheat the grill to 350°F using direct heat with a cast iron grate installed.

2. Season the bacon with the Sweet and Smoky Seasoning. Take each slice of bacon and carefully roll it up.

3. Insert toothpicks in an X shape to the bottom of the bacon roll up.

4. Put bacon roll ups on kamado grill and allow them to cook until finished. Make sure the bacon isn't too crispy.

5. If using real flower stems, remove the flowers from the stems carefully. You may need to use scissors. Insert half a toothpick into the top of the stem. Remove the toothpicks from the bacon roll up and insert onto stem toothpick.

6. If using wooden skewers, simply remove the toothpicks from the bacon roll up and insert onto skewer.

7. Whichever method you choose, you will likely need to use a ribbon to tie the stems/skewers together towards the top so they don't fall over and put them in a vase or wrap.

Chile Rubbed Grilled Pork Chops

Servings:8
Cooking Time: 8 Minutes

Ingredients:

- 4 boneless sirloin pork chops, about 6-oz each, 1⁄2 inch thick
- 2 cloves garlic, crushed
- 1 tablespoon ground cumin
- 1 teaspoon red pepper flakes
- 1⁄2 cup fresh lime juice
- 1⁄2 teaspoon salt
- 1⁄4 teaspoon black pepper, freshly ground
- 3 jalapeno Chile, seeded, very finely minced, about 1⁄4 cup
- 2 tablespoons sesame oil
- 2 tablespoons soy sauce
- 1/8 teaspoon sugar

Directions:

1. Stir together jalapeno, sesame oil, soy sauce and sugar together in a small bowl. Wearing disposable gloves, rub mixture over all surfaces of chops. Place chops in single layer in shallow dish. In a large measuring cup, stir together all marinade ingredients; pour over chops, set aside for 20-30 minutes.

2. Preheat the grill to 400°F using direct heat with a cast iron grate installed.

3. Remove chops from marinade, discarding marinade. Grill chops on grill, turning once, to medium doneness, about 3-4 minutes per side, until internal temperature on a thermometer reads 145°F, followed by a 3-minute rest time.

4. Best served with avocado-corn salsa!

Fresh Smoked Bacon

Servings: 8

Cooking Time: 210 Minutes

Ingredients:

- 1 skinned pork belly, about 4–5lb (1.8–2.3kg) in total
- for the cure
- 1⁄3 cup kosher salt
- 3 tbsp ground black pepper
- 2 tsp pink curing salt
- 1⁄3 cup packed light brown sugar, granulated sugar, or maple sugar or a mixture of all three
- to smoke
- hickory, oak, mesquite, or any fruit wood chunks

Directions:

1. To make the cure, in a large bowl, combine kosher salt, pepper, curing salt, and sugar. Rub the cure on both sides of pork belly. Place pork in an airtight container and cure for 5 days in the fridge, turning pork over each day.

2. Rinse pork and pat dry with paper towels. Refrigerate uncovered for at least 3 hours or overnight, turning once or twice.

3. Preheat the grill to 225°F (107°C). Once hot, add the wood chunks and install the heat deflector and standard grate. Place pork on the grate, close the lid, and smoke until the internal temperature reaches 165°F (74°C), about 2 to 3 hours.

4. Remove pork from the grill and cool as quickly as possible. (Use two pans with ice cubes between them, placing pork in the top pan.)Wrap tightly in plastic wrap and refrigerate overnight. Bacon can then be sliced and used as needed.

5. To cook the sliced bacon on the grate, preheat the grill to 375°F (191°C) using indirect heat with a cast iron grate or a cast iron griddle installed. Place bacon on the grate, close the lid, and grill until bacon reaches your desired texture, about 20 to 25 minutes.

Stir-fried Cucumber And Pork With Golden Garlic

Servings:2

Cooking Time: 5 Minutes

Ingredients:

* 1/2 cup (120 ml) peanut or vegetable oil
* 3 tbsp (45 ml) chopped garlic
* 12 ounces (340 g) lean pork shoulder or butt, cut into 1/4 inch (65 cm) thick bite-sized slices
* 1 1/2 tsp (8 ml) cornstarch
* 3 tsp (15 ml) soy sauce
* 1/4 tsp (1.5 ml) sugar
* 3/4 tsp (3.75 ml) salt
* 8 slices ginger, smashed
* 1 large English cucumber, ends trimmed, halved lengthwise and cut on the diagonal into 1/4 inch (65 cm) thick slices

Directions:

1. Preheat the grill to 600°F using direct heat with a cast iron grate installed. Once the kamado grill is steadily at this temperature, shut the bottom draft door and carefully open the lid.

2. Carbon Steel Wok, heat the pan until a bead of water vaporizes within 1 to 2 seconds of contact. Carefully add the oil and garlic and cook, stirring 30 seconds to 1 minute or until the garlic is light golden.

3. Remove the pan from the heat. Remove the garlic with a metal skimmer and put on a plate lined with paper towels. Carefully remove the oil from the woke and reserve. Wash the pan and dry it thoroughly.

4. In a shallow bowl combine the pork, cornstarch, 11/2 teaspoon (8 ml) of the soy sauce, sugar and 1/4 teaspoon (1.5 ml) of the salt. Ina small bowl combine the remaining 11/2 teaspoon

(8 ml) soy sauce and 1 tablespoon (15 ml) cold water.

5. Again, heat the wok over high heat until a beat of water vaporizes within 1 to 2 seconds of contact. Swirl in 2 tablespoons (30 ml) of the reserved garlic oil, add the ginger slices; then, using a spatula, stir-fry 30 seconds or until the ginger is fragrant. Push the ginger to the sides of the wok, carefully add the pork, and spread it evenly in one layer in the pan.

6. Cook undisturbed 1 minute, letting the pork begin to sear. Then stir-fry 1 minute or until the pork is lightly browned but now cooked through. Add the cucumber and stir-fry 30 seconds or until well combined. Sprinkle on the remaining 1/2 tsp (2.5 ml) salt, swirl the reserved soy sauce mixture into the pan and stir-fry 1 minute or until the pork is just cooked and the cucumber begins to wilt. Stir in the reserved garlic.

Championship Ribs

Servings:2

Cooking Time: 90 Minutes

Ingredients:

* 3 slabs of St. Louis-style ribs or baby back ribs, cut in half, membrane off* and ribs washed
* 1 cup of your favorite commercial or homemade dry BBQ rub
* 1 cup honey
* 1-1/2 cups apple juice
* 2 cups honey BBQ Sauce
* 1/2 cup salt
* 1/2 cup turbinado sugar
* 1/4 cup granulated brown sugar
* 1 tbsp granulated garlic
* 1 tbsp granulated onion
* 2 tbsp paprika
* 2 tbsp chili powder

- 2 tbsp freshly ground black pepper
- 2 tsp cayenne
- 1 tbsp thyme leaves
- 1 tbsp ground cumin
- 1 tsp ground nutmeg

Directions:

1. Cover the ribs with the rub, using about two-thirds on the meaty side and one-third on the boney side. Allow to stand at room temperature for 30 minutes before grilling.

2. Preheat the grill to 325°F using direct heat with a cast iron grate installed. Using a handful of hickory and cherry chips will help carmelize the ribs.

3. Cook for one-and-a-half hours, using a rib rack if you need it to have sufficient space for three slabs of ribs. Remove ribs to a flat pan or cookie sheet and brush them all on both sides with honey.

4. Put the ribs in an aluminum foil pan with about one-inch of apple juice in the bottom, standing them on end in the pan if necessary to get them to fit. Cover with foil and continue cooking for about one hour, replenishing the apple juice if needed to maintain liquid in the pan. Test the ribs by inserting a toothpick to determine whether they are tender.

5. At this point, you could cool them down, wrap each slab separately and refrigerate them for a day or two. They can then be transported to a tailgate party or reheated for entertaining at home.

6. When ready to serve them, transfer the cooked ribs to a medium hot grill. Brush with Honey BBQ Sauce; heat a few minutes, flipping them to heat both sides. Cut in to pieces and serve.

7. Removing the membrane: Carefully slide an implement, such as a fish skinner (available in the sporting goods department), the tip of a butter knife or the tip of a meat thermometer between the membrane and a bone near the end of the rack of ribs. Rock the implement back and forth gently to loosen the membrane until you have enough space to slide your finger under it. Using a paper towel, pull up the membrane and slowly peel the membrane off.

8. Combine all ingredients, mix well, and store in an airtight container.

Baby Back Ribs With Quince Barbecue Sauce

Servings:4
Cooking Time: 210 Minutes

Ingredients:

- 2 racks baby back ribs, membranes removed
- Sea salt
- Freshly ground black pepper
- Smoked paprika
- 1 cup apple cider, in a mister
- 8 oz. quince paste, cut into ½ inch pieces
- ⅓ cup dark rum
- ⅓ cup apple cider vinegar
- ¼ cup ketchup
- 3 tbsp fresh lime juice
- 1½ tbsp Worcestershire sauce
- ½ tsp cinnamon
- ½ tsp ground ginger
- ½ tsp nutmeg
- 2 tbsp honey
- Coarse salt and freshly ground black pepper
- ¼ cup water

Directions:

1. Preheat the grill to 275°F using direct heat with a cast iron grate installed.

2. Season the ribs on both sides with salt, pepper and paprika. Arrange the ribs bone side down on the cooking grid. Spray with the cider after the first hour. Cook the ribs until they're well-browned and tender enough to pull apart with your fingers, about 3 hours, spraying each hour with the cider. Brush the ribs on both sides with the barbecue sauce and continue cooking for 30 minutes. Serve immediately with the sauce on the side.

3. For the barbecue sauce, place the quince paste, rum, vinegar, ketchup, lime juice, Worcestershire sauce, cinnamon, ginger, nutmeg, honey, salt and pepper in a saucepan with ¼ cup water. Gently simmer over medium heat until thick, 10 minutes, whisking until smooth. The sauce should be thick but pourable.

Bacon Mac & Cheese

Servings:8
Cooking Time: 5 Minutes

Ingredients:
- 1 tablespoon olive oil
- 1 cup Panko (Japanese-style) breadcrumbs
- 12 slices flavorful smoked bacon
- 3 cups uncooked elbow macaroni
- ½ cup Cabot 2% Plain Greek-Style Yogurt or Cabot Plain Greek-Style Yogurt
- ¼ cup mayonnaise
- 8 ounces Cabot Extra Sharp Cheddar or Seriously Sharp Cheddar, grated (about 2 cups), plus more for garnish
- 2 tablespoons cider vinegar
- 1-2 teaspoons hot sauce
- 1 teaspoon Dijon mustard
- 1 medium clove garlic, coarsely chopped
- ½ teaspoon salt
- ½ teaspoon ground black pepper
- Optional extras

Directions:
1. Preheat the grill to 350°F using direct heat with a cast iron grate installed.

2. Heat oil on preheated Half Moon Cast Iron Griddle or a grill-safe pan. Add breadcrumbs and stir in pan until golden, about 1 1⁄2 minutes. immediately scrape into small bowl and set aside.

3. Add bacon to Half Moon Griddle and cook until crisp; transfer to paper towels to drain, then crumble or chop and set aside.

4. In large pot of boiling salted water, cook macaroni according to package directions until just tender. Drain and rinse under cold water until cool.

5. While macaroni cooks, combine yogurt and mayonnaise in blender; add cheddar, vinegar, hot sauce, mustard, garlic, salt and pepper; blend until the consistency of mayonnaise and nearly smooth, stirring and scraping down side of container as needed to help ingredients "liquefy".

6. In large bowl, toss together macaroni, cheddar dressing and bacon in large bowl, mixing well. Serve topped with additional cheese and toasted breadcrumbs. Surround with bowls of optional extras as desired.

7. Optional extras: sliced green onions, chopped Italian parsley, slivered fresh basil, raw fresh corn kernels, diced fresh tomatoes, diced bell peppers, thinly sliced romaine lettuce

Porchetta

Servings: 16
Cooking Time: 270 Minutes

Ingredients:

- 1 boneless, skin-on pork belly, about 8lb (3.6kg) in total
- 4 tbsp kosher salt
- 4 tbsp rice flour
- 4lb (1.8kg) unpeeled red potatoes, diced large
- for the rub
- 2 tbsp kosher salt
- 2 tbsp ground black pepper
- 3 tbsp ground fennel seed
- 3 tbsp ground cumin
- 1 tbsp crushed red pepper flakes
- 3 tbsp chopped fresh thyme
- 12 garlic cloves, minced
- to smoke
- apple, hickory, or cherry wood chunks

Directions:

1. To make the rub, in a medium bowl, combine all the rub ingredients. Place pork belly skin side down on a large cutting board. Use your hands to rub the mixture deeply into the cracks and crevices of the belly meat (not the skin).

2. Roll pork belly into a tight log and set aside, seam side down. Using kitchen twine, cut lengths long enough to tie around pork and cut enough strings to space about 1 inch (5cm) apart. Lay them down along a cutting board, about 1 inch (2.5cm) apart each. Place the rolled pork seam side down on top of the strings. Working from the outermost strings toward the center, tie up pork tightly.

3. Combine salt and rice flour. Rub the flour mixture over the entire surface of porchetta. Wrap tightly with plastic wrap and refrigerate overnight or up to 3 days. Before smoking, remove from the fridge and let come to room temperature.

4. Preheat the grill to 300°F (149°C) using indirect heat with a standard grate installed. Once hot, add the wood chunks, place pork in a V-rack, and set the rack in a drip pan. Place pork setup in the grill, close the lid, and roast until the internal temperature reaches 160°F, about 2 hours, basting with drippings every half hour.

5. After 1 hour of cooking, add potatoes to the drip pan and stir to coat. Continue roasting until a knife or skewer inserted into pork encounters very little resistance (aside from the outer layer of skin), about 2 more hours. Close the top and bottom vents to increase the temperature to 500°F (260°C) and continue roasting until the skin is completely crisp and potatoes are tender, about 20 to 30 minutes.

6. Remove pork from the grill and place on a cutting board tented with aluminum foil to rest for 15 minutes. Remove potatoes from drip pan and drain any excess fat. Season with salt and pepper to taste. Using a very sharp knife, slice the porchetta into disks about 3⁄4 inch (2cm) thick. Serve with roasted potatoes.

Smoked Andouille & Crawfish Gumbo

Servings: 12
Cooking Time: 180 Minutes

Ingredients:

- 1 green bell pepper, left whole
- 1 large yellow onion, halved
- 3 stalks of celery, left whole
- 1½ cups vegetable oil
- ½ cups all-purpose flour
- ½lb (225g) andouille sausage

- 1lb (450g) smoked sausage
- 8 cups chicken stock
- 1lb (450g) crawfish meat
- 1½ tsp kosher salt
- ½ tsp ground cayenne pepper (optional)
- 2 tbsp chopped fresh flat-leaf parsley
- 2 tbsp sliced scallions
- 6 cups cooked white rice, to serve (optional)

Directions:

1. Preheat the grill to 325°F (163°C) using direct heat with a cast iron grate installed and a dutch oven on the grate. Place pepper, onion, and celery on the grate around the dutch oven, close the grill lid, and grill until beginning to soften and char, about 6 to 8 minutes. Transfer the vegetables to a cutting board. Seed and dice the pepper, and dice the celery and onion. Set aside.

2. In the hot dutch oven, heat oil until shimmering. Add flour and stir. Close the grill lid and cook for 20 to 25 minutes, stirring every 5 minutes. While the roux cooks, place the sausages on the grate next to the dutch oven, close the grill lid, and grill until slightly charred, about 10 minutes. Remove the sausages from the grill, finely dice andouille and slice smoked sausage into bite-sized pieces.

3. Once the roux looks dark brown in color, add sausages, peppers, onions, and celery to the dutch oven, and stir to coat. Close the grill lid and cook until the vegetables are soft, about 8 to 10 minutes.

4. Add stock to the dutch oven, and stir until the roux and stock are well combined. Leaving the dutch oven uncovered, close the grill lid and reduce the heat by closing the top and bottom vents most of the way. Cook for 90 minutes, stirring occasionally. Add crawfish to the dutch oven, close the grill lid, and cook for 15 minutes more.

5. Remove the dutch oven from the grill and let sit for 5 minutes before skimming any fat that has risen to the surface. Stir in salt and cayenne (if using). Taste and adjust the seasonings as needed. Stir in parsley and scallions, and serve immediately with white rice (if using).

Brunswick Stew

Servings:8
Cooking Time: 120 Minutes

Ingredients:
- 2 lbs. precooked pulled pork
- 2 lbs. chicken breast
- 1 28 oz. can crushed tomatoes
- 32 oz. chicken broth
- 1 package frozen lima beans
- 1 lb. shoe peg corn
- 1/2 lb. red potatoes cut in half
- 1 tbsp garlic salt
- 2 garlic cloves, minced
- ½ yellow onion, diced
- 2 tsp kosher salt
- 1 tbsp olive oil
- ¼ cup Bold & Tangy Carolina Style BBQ sauce

Directions:

1. Preheat the grill to 300°F using direct heat with a cast iron grate installed.

2. In your dutch oven with olive oil, sear and cook the chicken breast, remove and cut into cubes and put back into the dutch oven.

3. Add all the other ingredients and mix. Cook for approximately two hours. Serve with cornbread, or biscuits.

Adobo Chicken Wings

Servings: 21

Cooking Time: 150 Minutes

Ingredients:

- 42 chicken wings, about 5lb (2.3kg) in total
- 3 cups rice flour
- 3 tbsp ancho chili powder
- 3 tsp kosher salt
- 6 tbsp chopped fresh cilantro, for garnish
- for the pickles
- 1⁄4 cup sugar
- 1⁄2 cup white vinegar
- 2 tbsp pickling spice
- 3 large red bell peppers, cut into 11⁄2-in (3.75-cm) strips
- for the glaze
- 6 chipotle peppers in adobo
- 3 tbsp adobo sauce
- 2 cups honey
- 6 tbsp fresh lime juice
- 6 tbsp soy sauce
- for the crema
- 2 avocados, halved and pitted
- 4 tbsp lime juice or to taste
- 2 cups Mexican crema or sour cream
- kosher salt and freshly ground black pepper
- to smoke
- maple or apricot wood chunks

Directions:

1. To make the pickles, in a small saucepan on the stovetop, combine sugar, vinegar, and pickling spice. Bring to a boil over high heat, then reduce heat and simmer for 5 minutes. Bring a separate saucepan of water to boil and blanch the red bell peppers by submerging them in the boiling water for 2 minutes. Pack the peppers in one or two glass jars. Pour the pickling solution over peppers to fill the jars and seal the jars with lids. Refrigerate for at least 1 day.

2. Pat chicken dry with paper towels. Place in a large bowl, sprinkle with rice flour, chili powder, and salt, and toss to coat. Arrange wings in a single layer on a wire rack placed on a baking pan. Refrigerate uncovered for 8 hours.

3. Preheat the grill to 250°F (121°C). Once hot, add the wood chunks and install the heat deflector and a multi-tiered rack. Arrange wings on the rack, close the lid, and smoke until the internal temperature reaches 165°F (74°C), about 2 hours. Remove wings from the grill and let rest for 1 hour.

4. To make the glaze, in a blender, combine peppers, adobo sauce, honey, lime juice, and soy sauce, and purée until smooth. Pour into a small bowl and set aside.

5. Reconfigure the grill for direct heat and install a cast iron grate. Open the top and bottom vents to raise the grill temperature to 400°F (204°C). To make the crema, place avocados cut side down on the grate. Grill until char marks form, about 7 to 10 minutes. Scoop the avocado flesh into a food processor, add lime juice and crema, and process until smooth. Season with salt and pepper to taste.

6. Place wings on the grate and grill until the skin is crisp and grill marks appear, about 2 to 3 minutes per side. Transfer to a serving dish and toss with sauce to coat. Sprinkle with cilantro and serve with the pickles and crema.

Prosciutto Wrapped Cheese Dogs

Servings:6
Cooking Time: 12 Minutes

Ingredients:

- 6 Nature's Own 100% Whole Wheat Hot Dog Rolls
- 1 teaspoon Italian seasoning
- 3 pieces string cheese
- 6 prosciutto slices
- 2 teaspoons olive oil
- 6 fat-free hot dogs
- Dijon mustard
- Chopped tomato

Directions:

1. Preheat the grill to 375°F using direct heat with a cast iron grate installed.

2. Cut a lengthwise slit down center of each hot dog; do not cut all the way through bottom or ends. Sprinkle Italian seasoning evenly over hot dogs, rolling to coat.

3. Pull each string cheese piece in half vertically, forming 6 pieces. Stuff 1 cheese piece into each hot dog slit. Wrap 1 prosciutto slice around each stuffed hot dog, encasing completely. Brush prosciutto lightly with oil. Place hot dogs on baking sheet.

4. Cook 10 to 12 minutes or until heated through and cheese melts. Place hot dogs in rolls. Top with mustard, tomato and basil.

Honey Pork Tenderloin Kabob

Servings:4
Cooking Time: 10 Minutes

Ingredients:

- ½ cup bourbon or 2 tablespoons cider vinegar
- ½ cup honey
- ½ cup mustard
- 1 teaspoon dried tarragon
- 3 to 4 sweet potatoes, cut into 24 one inch cubes
- 1½ pounds pork tenderloin, cut into 24 one-inch cubes
- 4 medium ripe peaches, unpeeled, pitted and quartered
- 4 green bell peppers, each cut into 8 two-inch pieces
- 8 yellow onion, each cut into 4 two-inch pieces
- Olive oil, for grilling

Directions:

1. Preheat the grill to 400°F using direct heat with a cast iron grate installed.

2. Mix first four ingredients in a bowl; stir well and set glaze aside. Grill, steam or boil sweet potatoes until crisp-tender. Thread 3 sweet potato cubes, 3 pork cubes, 2 peach quarters, 4 green pepper pieces and 4 onion pieces alternately onto each of eight Flexible Skewers.

3. Brush kabobs with honey glaze mixture; lightly oil cooking grid. Grill for 5 minutes on each side or until thoroughly cooked, basting occasionally with glaze.

4. Bourbon is optional, can substitute 2 tablespoons cider vinegar

Country Christmas

Servings:12
Cooking Time: 280 Minutes

Ingredients:

- 1 ham, 10-12 lbs
- 1 20 oz. can round sliced pineapple
- 1 jar maraschino cherries
- 2 boxes brown sugar
- 24 oz whole white mushrooms

- 1 package Italian sausage (5 links)
- 1 package extra sharp cheddar cheese, cut into small cubes
- 4-6 garlic cloves, finely chopped
- Dried parsley
- 29oz. cans of peaches with heavy syrup
- 1 cup pineapple bits
- ½ cup tapioca
- 1 box cake mix
- 1 ¼ cup brown sugar
- ¼ stick unsalted butter
- Dutch Oven
- 3 cups corn meal
- 1 egg
- 2 ¼ cups buttermilk
- ½ cup canola oil
- 6-8 bunches collards
- 2 large sweet yellow onions, chopped
- 4-6 garlic cloves, chopped
- 8-10 smoked turkey butts
- 3-4 turnip roots, chopped
- ¼ cup crushed red pepper
- ½ tbsp kosher salt
- ½ tbsp black pepper
- ½ tbsp cayenne pepper
- ¼ ts habanero pepper
- Jacks Old South or your favorite rub
- Garlic powder
- 2 large shallots, chopped

Directions:

1. Preheat the grill to 350°F using direct heat with a cast iron grate installed. Line a 9×13 baking pan with aluminum foil.

2. Rinse ham with cold water, pat dry, and set aside. Take the juice from the pineapple and mix well with the brown sugar to make a nice thick syrupy glaze. Next add the pineapple to the ham putting a cherry in the hole of each pineapple round. Then pour the glaze over the ham.

3. Loosely cover the ham with aluminum foil and cook for 3-4 hours basting the ham with the pan juice every 30 min.

4. Let stand for 30 minutes, slice and enjoy.

5. Preheat the grill to 350°F using direct heat with a cast iron grate installed.

6. Clean mushrooms under running water. Pat dry, remove stems and brush with olive oil.

7. Cook the sausage on the kamado grill for 30-45 min until done (160 degree internal temp). Remove sausage and let cool then finely chop.

8. Stuff each mushroom with the sausage first, then top with garlic, then add the cube of cheese, then a sprinkle of parsley. Place mushrooms on a perforated grid and cook for 30 minutes. Remove and let cool for 5 minutes.

9. Set the kamado grill up for indirect cooking at 350°F.

10. Pour the 2 cans of peaches with heavy syrup into a seasoned dutch oven. Next, pour in pineapple tidbits over peaches. Then add the tapioca over the pineapple. Follow this with the cake mix and then brown sugar. Top the brown sugar with thinly sliced unsalted butter.

11. Place lid on dutch oven and cook for 45 minutes. Remove from kamado grill let cool for 15 minutes.

12. Preheat the grill to 350°F using direct heat with a cast iron grate installed.

13. In a large bowl mix the cornmeal, egg, buttermilk, and sugar. You are looking for a nice firm consistency; not dry or too wet (Remember you can add but you can't take away). Add oil to the skillet and let it get hot (about 15 minutes). Then add the ½ cup canola oil to the cornbread mixture and mix. Pour the cornbread mixture

into the skillet and cook for 30 minutes or until golden brown.

14. Let cool for 15 minutes and enjoy.

15. Preheat the grill to 350°F using direct heat with a cast iron grate installed.

16. In a dutch oven add all of the ingredients except the collards. Cover with water making sure to cover the turkey butts (about 8 cups). Boil down by half or until the turkey butts are falling off the bone. Remove turkey butts and when cool remove the meat and discard the bones. Place turkey meat back in Dutch Oven. At this point it is important to taste your base to make sure it is to your satisfaction.

17. Slowly add the collards to the base using a wooden spoon to work the greens. Note: Do not add additional water during this process – let the greens cook down (about 30 minutes). Continue to add greens using the same method until all of the greens are in the Dutch Oven. Cook for an additional 90 minutes and check for tenderness.

18. Enjoy.

Cuban Pork (lechon Asado)

Servings: 8
Cooking Time: 840 Minutes

Ingredients:

- 1 (7-9 lb) pork shoulder
- 1 recipe Cuban Mojo

Directions:

1. Score the skin and fat on the pork shoulder by cutting in one direction, then the other to form cross hatches.

2. Pour Cuban Mojo over the pork shoulder, cover, and refrigerate at least four hours, preferably overnight, turning once.

3. Remove the pork from the marinade 30 minutes before cooking.

4. Grilling:

5. Preheat the grill to 225°F using direct heat with a cast iron grate installed, placing the plate setter and grid inside.

6. Place the pork shoulder on the grid and close the dome. The grill is designed to maintain this temperature for up to 18 hours.

7. After 10 hours, check the internal temperature of the pork. Remove the roast when it reads 200°F.

8. Carefully remove the pork shoulder from the grill and allow it to rest 30 minutes before slicing/pulling it apart.

Sriracha Pork Chops

Servings:4
Cooking Time: 9 Minutes

Ingredients:

- 4 (1") boneless pork chops
- 2 Tablespoons Better Than Bouillon Reduced Sodium Roasted Chicken Base
- 1 Tablespoon minced garlic
- 1 Tablespoon Sriracha sauce
- 1 Tablespoon freshly chopped cilantro
- 1 Tablespoon freshly squeezed lime juice
- 1/4 cup brown sugar
- 2 teaspoons freshly minced ginger

Directions:

1. Instructions Mix the Roasted Chicken Base, garlic, sriracha, cilantro, lime juice, brown sugar and ginger in a small mixing bowl. Add half of the mixture to a resealable plastic bag and add the pork chops and refrigerate for at least 3 hours and up to 8 hours.

2. Reserve the rest of the marinade, covered and refrigerated until ready to use.

3. Preheat the grill to 425°F using direct heat with a cast iron grate installed.

4. Remove the pork chops from the marinade and place directly onto the grill. Grill for 4 minutes. Using tongs, turn the pork chops and brush with the reserved marinade. Grill for an additional 4 – 5 minutes.

5. Remove the pork chops from the kamado grill and brush with the reserved marinade before serving.

6. Serve immediately.

Famous Dave's Five Star Bbq Sticky Ribs

Servings:6
Cooking Time: 120 Minutes

Ingredients:

- 4 racks loin back ribs
- 1/2 cup (120 ml) melted hickory bacon grease
- Yellow mustard
- BBQ Sticky Ribs Marinade, Rib Rub and Frosting
- 2 cans frozen apple juice concentrate, prepared with 2 cans of purified water
- 4 Tbsp (72 g) canning salt (Dave prefers Morton's green box)
- 3 Tbsp (45 ml) Wright's Liquid Smoke
- 4 Tbsp (60 ml) Frank's Hot Sauce
- 1/2 cup (120 ml) fine sea salt
- 1/4 cup (60 ml) Kosher salt
- 1/3 cup (80 ml) Maple sugar
- 1/3 cup (80 ml) dark brown sugar
- 1/4 cup (60 ml) Turbinado raw sugar
- 2 tbsp (30 ml) granulated onion powder
- 1 tbsp (15 ml) granulated garlic
- 1 tbsp (15 ml) paprika
- 1 tbsp (15 ml) fresh ground pepper
- 2 tsp (10 ml) celery seed
- 2 tsp (10 ml) dry rosemary (grind in coffee grinder)
- 1 tsp (5 ml) cayenne pepper
- 2 cups (475 ml) Famous Dave's Rich & Sassy BBQ Sauce
- 2 cups (475 ml) Open Pit BBQ Sauce
- 1/2 cup (120 ml) dark brown sugar
- 12 oz (355 ml) Smucker's Apricot Preserves
- 1/4 cup (60 ml) Frank's Hot Sauce
- 2 oz (60 ml) Kahlua Liqueur
- 1/2 oz (15 g) semi sweet chocolate

Directions:

1. Prepare ribs by pulling the membrane off the bone side. Start on the small end of the rack and work your thumb under the membrane (or use a butter knife). Once you have enough membrane to get a firm grip…grab it with a paper towel, and in one good pull jerk the membrane off the rack.

2. Prepare BBQ Sticky Ribs Marinade. Place one rack in each of four separate resealable bags with marinade. Be careful the sharp ends of the bones don't puncture the bags. Seal the bags and place in the refrigerator for 12 hours.

3. At 7 hours turn ribs over; at 12 hours remove ribs from marinade and rinse under cold water; pat dry with paper towels. Rub both sides of ribs with a light coating of yellow mustard. Dust ribs evenly with Rib Rub and set for one hour to let the juices start mixing with seasonings.

4. Preheat the grill to 250°F using direct heat with a cast iron grate installed. Place soaked hickory, apple or cherry wood chips on the charcoal. Place a Drip Pan on the platesetter and fill with 2 inches (5 cm) apple juice. Drizzle the ribs with melted hickory bacon grease and place on grate. After 2 hours, remove ribs; they should be a beautiful mahogany color.

5. Cover a sheet pan with aluminum foil. Place ribs on the foil and generously brush ribs with BBQ Sticky Ribs Frosting. Pour 1/2 cup (120 ml)

apple juice into the bottom of the sheet pan. Next, create a foil tent over the ribs making sure the ribs do not touch the top of the foil. Place pan back in the kamado grill and cook 1 1/2 to 2 hours at 300°F until the ribs are tender. When you pick ribs up with your tongs, they should bend easily. Re-foil ribs and keep covered with a heavy towel to keep warm until you are ready to caramelize the sauce on your ribs. You do not want the ribs to be sitting out and losing their moisture.

6. While the ribs are resting, raise the temperature of the kamado grill to 600°F. You will need a hot grid to caramelize sauce on ribs. Baste ribs with sauce and place on hot cooking grid Once the sauce starts to caramelize, turn over and slather with more sauce. With this last step, you are charring the sauce and building up layers of delicious flavors on your ribs. Don't over-char your ribs or they will taste burnt. When the ribs look beautifully caramelized, remove them from your grill. Slice into single bones and serve with extra sauce.

7. Mix ingredients together and equally divide into 4 two-gallon bags (turkey roasting bags work, too.)

8. In a bowl, add all ingredients and blend together.

9. In a pan, add all ingredients. Blend together and heat up until the sauce simmers and the chocolate melts and is incorporated into the sauce. Remove from heat and cool. I call my BBQ sauce "Frosting" because it's so tasty you'll want to lick it all up!

Chili Crusted Boar Ham

Servings:6
Cooking Time: 240 Minutes

Ingredients:

- Heavy duty disposable roasting pan
- 1 wild boar ham (regular ham can be used)
- 6 oz chili powder
- 1 Tablespoon granulated garlic
- 1 Tablespoon onion powder
- 2 Tablespoons cumin
- 4 Tablespoons dark brown sugar
- 12 oz can of Coca-Cola

Directions:

1. Preheat the grill to 300°F using direct heat with a cast iron grate installed.

2. Place the ham in a Drip Pan. Combine all of the dry seasonings including the brown sugar and mix until they are mixed well. Pat the seasoning blend liberally onto the ham, covering it completely on all sides. Pour the Coca-Cola into the pan (but not over the ham) and cover very tightly with foil.

3. Place pan on cooking grid and bake for 4 hours or until tender. Do not open the foil while cooking. Remove from the kamado grill and let cool; shred with Meat Claws and serve as sandwiches with Amy's Coleslaw.

Beer-infused Baby Back Ribs

Servings: 2
Cooking Time: 300 Minutes

Ingredients:

- 1 rack of baby back ribs, about 3lb (1.4kg) in total
- BBQ sauce, to serve
- for the brine
- 3/4 cup kosher salt
- 1/3 cup packed light brown sugar
- 1/3 cup raw sugar
- 1 1/2 tsp pink curing salt
- 3 cups hot water
- 2 cups beer, preferably brown ale or lager

- 2 tbsp pickling spice
- to smoke
- apple or apricot wood chunks

Directions:

1. To make the brine, in a large bowl, whisk together kosher salt, brown sugar, raw sugar, pink curing salt, and hot water until sugars and salts dissolve. Whisk in beer and pickling spice, and set aside to cool to room temperature.

2. Place ribs on a cutting board and remove the thin, papery membrane from the back of the ribs. Cut the rack in half widthwise between the middle bones. Place ribs in a heavy-duty resealable plastic bag and add brine to cover. Squeeze out any excess air and place in an aluminum pan or a roasting pan. (Any extra brine can be refrigerated and saved for a later use.) Refrigerate for 24 hours.

3. Remove ribs from the brine and pat dry with paper towels. Arrange ribs on a wire rack over a rimmed baking sheet and let dry uncovered in the fridge for 2 hours.

4. Preheat the grill to 225°F (107°C). Once hot, add the wood chunks and install the heat deflector and a standard grate. Place ribs bone side down on the grate, close the lid, and smoke until the meat shrinks back from the ends of the bones by 1⁄2 inch (1.25cm), about 4 to 5 hours. Transfer ribs to a cutting board and cut into individual ribs.

5. Place ribs on a serving platter, brush with BBQ sauce, and serve immediately. (For more charring and caramelization, return the sauce-coated ribs to the grill for 5 to 10 minutes more before serving.)

Pig Candy

Servings:6

Cooking Time: 20 Minutes

Ingredients:

- 1 cup brown sugar
- 1⁄2 tsp cayenne pepper
- 1 lb thick cut bacon
- 1⁄2 cup maple syrup

Directions:

1. Preheat the grill to 350°F using direct heat with a cast iron grate installed. Cover a baking sheet in foil, and place a wire rack on the baking sheet, or use a Half Moon Perforated Cooking Grid.

2. Mix together brown sugar and cayenne pepper in a small bowl. Cover strips of bacon with brown sugar mixture. Then, place the bacon on the wire rack or cooking grid.

3. Place baking sheet in the kamado grill and allow to cook until the bacon starts to crisp. Then brush the top of the bacon with maple syrup, flip the bacon and brush the other side with maple syrup as well. Allow to continue to cook until it is to your preference of doneness. Remove and serve.

4. You may serve it with a small side of additional maple syrup for dipping if you'd like it to be extra sweet!

Spicy Bbq Spare Ribs

Servings: 6
Cooking Time: 240 Minutes

Ingredients:

- 6lb (2.7kg) spare ribs, trimmed and membrane removed
- for the marinade
- 1 cup cider vinegar
- 1 cup apple cider
- 4 garlic cloves, minced
- 2 bay leaves

- 2 tbsp hot sauce
- 1 tbsp kosher salt
- for the sauce
- 3⁄4 cup apple cider vinegar
- 3⁄4 cups apple cider
- 1 tbsp hot sauce
- for the rub
- 1⁄2 cup packed light brown sugar
- 3 tbsp chili powder
- 1 tbsp smoked paprika
- 2 tbsp granulated garlic
- 2 tbsp onion powder
- 1 tsp ground cayenne pepper
- 1 tbsp kosher salt
- 2 tsp ground cumin
- 1⁄2 tsp ground cinnamon
- 1 tsp ground black pepper
- to smoke
- pecan wood chunks

Directions:

1. To make the marinade, in a shallow nonreactive pan large enough to hold ribs, combine vinegar, cider, garlic, bay leaves, hot sauce, and salt. Place ribs in the marinade, turn to coat, and cover with plastic wrap. Refrigerate for 8 hours or up to 16 hours, turning once. Before grilling, remove ribs from the marinade and allow to come to room temperature.

2. To make the rub, in a medium bowl, combine all the rub ingredients. Sprinkle the ribs all over with 1⁄2 cup rub, patting it on with your fingers. Wrap tightly with plastic wrap and refrigerate for 90 minutes.

3. Preheat the grill to 300°F (149°C). Once hot, add the wood chunks and install the heat deflector and a multi-tiered rack.

4. To make the sauce, in a medium bowl, whisk together vinegar, cider, and hot sauce. Place ribs flat on the rack, close the lid, and smoke until the edges are crispy and the meat has pulled back from the bone, about 3 to 4 hours. Brush with the sauce every hour, and turn once during grilling.

5. Remove ribs from the grill, brush with any remaining sauce, and serve immediately.

Braised Carnitas With Chimichurri Sauce

Servings:8
Cooking Time: 300 Minutes

Ingredients:

- 4 lbs. boneless pork shoulder
- 3 tbsp olive oil
- 1 can of Coca-Cola
- 2 oranges, juiced
- 6 limes, 2 juiced and 4 sliced in wedges for serving
- 2 jalapeños, seeded and chopped
- 1 yellow onion, diced
- 2 tbsp garlic, minced
- Flour tortillas
- 2 tbsp oregano
- 3 tsp cumin
- 3 tbsp olive oil
- 3 tbsp salt
- 3 tbsp pepper
- 3 tsp. minced garlic
- 1⁄2 tbsp. salt (more to taste if needed)
- 2 cups cilantro, finely chopped
- 3 tbsp oregano
- 1 cup parsley, finely chopped
- 1⁄4 cup minced red onion
- 1 lime, juiced
- 2 tbsp. white wine vinegar
- 1 cup EVOO

Directions:

1. Preheat the grill to 400°F using direct heat with a cast iron grate installed.

2. Rinse pork and pat dry. Season the entire pork shoulder liberally with the rub.

3. Place a dutch oven on the grid and add the oil to heat. Add the pork shoulder and sear on all sides until lightly browned.

4. Remove the dutch oven from the grill. Add the platesetter for indirect cooking and stabilize the kamado grill at 300°F.

5. Arrange the shoulder in the dutch oven with the fat cap facing up. Pour the Coca-Cola, orange juice and lime juice into the dutch oven. Add the jalapeños, onion and garlic over the top of the pork. Cook for 4 ½ to 5 hours until meat pulls apart easily.

6. Mix all the ingredients together.

7. Crush the garlic and salt together to make a paste. Add cilantro, oregano, parsley, red onion and lime juice until combined. Add white wine vinegar and EVOO, mix and add salt/pepper to taste. Serve over the carnitas with tortillas.

Carolina Pulled Pork

Servings: 20
Cooking Time: 480 Minutes

Ingredients:
- 10lb (4.5kg) boneless pork shoulder
- 20 sandwich buns, to serve
- for the rub
- 4 tbsp paprika
- 2 tbsp ground black pepper
- 4 tsp ground cayenne pepper
- for the coleslaw
- 1/2 cup mayonnaise
- 3 tbsp apple cider vinegar
- 1 tbsp sugar
- 1 tbsp celery seed
- 1 head of napa cabbage, shredded
- 2 large carrots, shredded
- for the sauce
- 1 cup bourbon
- 4 tbsp molasses
- 3 cups malt vinegar
- 2 cups water
- 4 dried chipotle peppers, rehydrated and chopped
- 4 tbsp kosher salt
- 2 tbsp crushed red pepper flakes
- 2 tbsp ground black pepper
- 4 tsp ground cayenne pepper
- to smoke
- hickory or oak wood chunks

Directions:

1. To make the rub, in a small bowl, combine paprika, pepper, and cayenne. Place pork on a baking pan and rub the mixture over all surfaces. Cover with plastic wrap and refrigerate for 24 hours.

2. To make the coleslaw, in a large bowl, whisk together mayonnaise, vinegar, sugar, and celery seed until well combined. Add cabbage and carrots, and toss to coat. Cover with plastic wrap and refrigerate for at least 4 hours.

3. Preheat the grill to 275°F (135°C). Once hot, add the wood chunks and install the heat deflector and a standard grate. Place pork on a V-rack over a drip pan and place on the grate. Close the lid and smoke until the internal temperature reaches 190°F (88°C), about 6 to 8 hours.

4. To make the sauce, in a saucepan, combine all the sauce ingredients and place the pan on the stovetop over medium heat. Simmer for 5 minutes. During the last 2 hours of smoking, baste pork with the sauce every 20 to 30 minutes.

Keep any sauce in the pan that remains after basting.

5. Transfer pork to a large platter to rest. Remove the drip pan and add the accumulated drippings to the saucepan with the remaining sauce. Heat on the stovetop over medium heat until warm, about 5 minutes.

6. Remove pork from the grill and shred, discarding any large pieces of fat and adding the sauce as desired. Pile pork on sandwich buns and top with coleslaw.

Herb-crusted Pork Short Ribs

Servings:6
Cooking Time: 20 Minutes

Ingredients:

- 3-4 lbs. Kurobuta Pork Short Ribs
- ½ cup Dijon mustard
- ½ cup thyme, dried
- 6 Tbsp rosemary, dried
- 2 Tbsp oregano, dried
- 2 Tbsp Kosher salt
- 1 Tbsp black pepper
- 10 cloves garlic
- ¾ cup honey
- Juice of 3 lemons

Directions:

1. In a mortar and pestle, crush garlic with herbs, salt and pepper to form a paste. Rub ribs completely with mustard. Covering all sides will ensure that crust adheres to the meat. Cover meat generously with herb paste, pressing gently into the meat. Place ribs in the refrigerator for 45 minutes before cooking.

2. In a small bowl, mix honey and lemon juice together.

3. Preheat the grill to 325°F using direct heat with a cast iron grate installed. Place ribs on opposite side of the charcoal to cook. When ribs reach 180°F, brush them with honey mixture. Remove ribs when they reach an internal temperature of 195°F. Brush once again with honey and lemon. Rest 15 minutes before slicing and serving.

Apple Cinnamon Pork Chops

Servings:4
Cooking Time: 20 Minutes

Ingredients:

- 4 bone-in ribeye (rib) pork chops, about ¾ inch thick
- Salt and pepper
- 3 tablespoons butter, divided
- 2 apples, peeled, cored and thinly sliced
- 1 large white onion, halved and thinly sliced
- 2 tablespoons brown sugar, packed
- 2 teaspoons cinnamon
- Pinch cayenne
- ⅔ cup apple cider
- ⅓ cup heavy cream

Directions:

1. Preheat the grill to 400°F using direct heat with a cast iron grate installed.

2. Generously season the chops with salt and pepper on both sides. Set aside.

3. In the Half Moon Cast Iron Griddle melt 2 tablespoons of butter. Immediately add the pork chops and cook until brown, about 3 minutes per side. Transfer to a plate and set aside.

4. In the Half Moon Cast Iron Griddle, still at 400°F, melt 1 tablespoon of butter. Immediately add the apples and onion and let them cook, until the onion is translucent, about 5 minutes. Stir in the brown sugar, cinnamon and cayenne. Next, stir in the apple cider and cream. Then add the pork chops, nestling them into the liquid, and

cook until the internal temperature of the pork reaches between 145°F. for medium rare and 160°F for medium. It should take about 3-4 minutes per side.

5. Serve the chops with the apple mixture spooned on top.

Charlotte Pork Chops

Servings:4
Cooking Time: 15 Minutes

Ingredients:

- 4 boneless pork chops, about ½ inch thick
- 4 medium yellow onions, halved and sliced thin
- 2 cloves garlic, crushed
- Vegetable oil
- BBQ rub
- 4 hamburger buns

Directions:

1. Preheat the grill to 400°F using direct heat with a cast iron grate installed.

2. Add the half cast iron griddle to one side to preheat. Season the chops with the barbecue rub. Add 1 to 2 tablespoons oil to the hot griddle and then add the onions. Season the onions with barbecue rub and sprinkle the garlic powder the top.

3. Cook for about 5 minutes tossing the onions occasionally. Add the pork chops and cook 3 to 4 minutes until golden broiwn. Flip and continue tossing the onions occasionally. Cook another 3 to 4 minutes until the chops are golden brown and have reached an internal temp of 150°F.

4. Remove the chops and onions from the grill. Place a chop on each bun and top with ¼ of the onions.

Pork Cacciatore

Servings:4
Cooking Time: 122 Minutes

Ingredients:

- 6 pounds boneless pork shoulder
- 1 1⁄4 teaspoon sea salt
- 3⁄4 teaspoon freshly ground pepper
- 2 tablespoons olive oil
- 1 large red bell pepper, sliced
- 1 large green bell pepper, sliced
- 2 yellow onions, sliced
- 3-4 cloves garlic, chopped
- 2 teaspoons dried basil
- 2 teaspoons dried parsley
- 1 teaspoon dried thyme
- 1 teaspoon red pepper flakes, optional
- 1 cup low sodium chicken broth
- 1 28 ounce can petite diced tomatoes
- 3 tablespoons tomato paste

Directions:

1. Preheat the grill to 350°F using direct heat with a cast iron grate installed.

2. Take pork shoulder out of package and wipe down with a paper towel. Season with salt and pepper.

3. Heat your dutch oven in the grill. Add in oil and let it get nice and hot. Add in pork and sear all sides for about 2 minutes; you want to create a nice sear. Add in peppers, onions and garlic. Cook for about 5 minutes stirring around using a wooden spoon.

4. Add in basil, parsley, thyme and red pepper flakes. Pour in chicken broth and diced tomatoes. Stir to incorporate all of the ingredients. Add in tomato paste and press against the pan with the back of your spoon to help incorporate into the liquid. Cover and let cook 2 hours.

5. Remove from grill. Use a large spoon and skim off the fat then go ahead and pull apart the pork or serve in large chunks with the peppers and onions. Enjoy!

Stuffed Pork Chops With Poblano Cream Sauce

Servings:4

Cooking Time: 32 Minutes

Ingredients:

- 4 double-cut pork chops
- 1 tablespoon olive oil
- 4 tablespoons Sweet & Smoky Seasoning
- 1 cup firmly packed Double Corn Cornbread, or store-bought
- ½ cup chopped smoked chorizo sausage
- ½ cup chopped fresh cilantro
- ½ cup ham or chicken stock
- 2 poblano peppers
- 1 teaspoon minced garlic
- ½ cup ham or chicken stock
- 1½ cups heavy cream
- ¼ cup yellow cornmeal
- 1 tablespoon freshly squeezed lime juice
- ½ cup chopped fresh cilantro

Directions:

1. Preheat the grill to 450°F using direct heat with a cast iron grate installed.

2. Using a paring knife, cut a 1½ to 2-inch-long pocket along the meat side of each pork chop. Season each pork chop with olive oil and 1 tablespoon of the rub. Crumble the cornbread into a small bowl, add the chorizo, cilantro and stock, and mix well. Divide the stuffing into quarters and place one-quarter of the stuffing inside the pocket of each pork chop.

3. Place the pork chops on the grid. Close the lid of the kamado grill and grill for 3 minutes on each side. Close the top and bottom vents, and roast the chops for 12 to 15 minutes, until a food thermometer registers 145°F or the desired doneness.

4. Transfer the pork chops to a platter, top with the sauce, and serve immediately.

5. Place the poblano peppers on the direct side of the grid. Close the lid of the kamado grill and cook, turning occasionally, for 3 to 5 minutes, until the peppers are black on all sides. Transfer the peppers to a resealable plastic bag. Seal the bag and let the peppers steam for 5 minutes. Remove the peppers from the bag and place on a cutting board. Using a paring knife, cut the peppers open lengthwise and remove and discard the seeds. Dice the peppers into small pieces.

6. Combine the peppers, garlic, stock, and cream in a small saucepan on the stovetop and simmer for 15 minutes. Using a whisk, add the cornmeal and continue to cook for 7 minutes, or until the sauce has thickened. Remove the saucepan from the heat and add the lime juice and cilantro. Keep warm.

Takeo Spikes' Ribs

Servings:4

Cooking Time: 130 Minutes

Ingredients:

- Ribs
- Your favorite BBQ Rub
- Yellow mustard
- Apple juice

Directions:

1. Take ribs out of the fridge and begin prep work. This will take about 30 minutes to an hour.

2. Remove the membrane, which is a thick plastic-like skin over the boney part of the ribs. Removing this allows the smoke to penetrate the meat better. Pry up on the membrane using a knife or other sharp utensil. Then grab the membrane with a paper towel and pull it clean off.
3. Then I apply a light coating of yellow hot dog mustard to the bony side of the ribs to help the rub to stick real good. Once the bony or bottom side of the ribs are coated with mustard and rub. I flip them over and do the same with the top side. Light coat of mustard then sprinkle on the rub. Not too thick but enough to cover the ribs real good. Once the ribs are coated on both sides with rub and mustard, I leave them there to go get the kamado grill ready.
4. Make sure you have plenty of lump charcoal in the fire bowl. I like to have it up to the top of the bowl, which is an inch or two above the air holes. Place the platesetter in place with the legs facing up then place the grate on top of that. If you are worried about the drippings on your platesetter, you can place a drip pan on it or some foil which can be easily thrown away when you're finished cooking.
5. After the coals have been burning for about 7 minutes, close the dome and leave the bottom and top vents all the way open until the kamado grill reaches about 230°F. While the kamado grill is heating up, go ahead and get the ribs and place them on the grate bone side down.
6. Once the kamado grill reaches 230°F, adjust the vent at the bottom and the top to hold this temperature. For me, that means the daisy wheel at the top is only slightly cracked open at about 20% open and the bottom vent is open about ¾ of an inch or so.

7. This is where the 2-2-1 method of making the ribs tender really starts. Start a timer or just make note of the time because the ribs will only stay in this current configuration for 2 hours.
8. Once 2 hours are up, the ribs should be wrapped in heavy duty foil or an easier method is to place them in a large foil pan with foil covering the top tightly. Then place back on the grill. Some folks put (only a little) apple juice down in the pan to create more steam and flavors. It is this steaming action that super tenderizes the ribs.
9. This is the 2nd step in the 2-2-1 method and lasts 2 hours, just like the first step. After 2 hours have expired with the ribs in foil or in the covered pan, remove them from the pan or foil and place them once again directly on the grates for 1 hour.
10. When they come out of the foil or pan, they look wet and there is no crust to speak of. The last hour on the grates dries the top a little and develops the crust on the outside that is usually desired. This is the last step and when the hour is up, the ribs are ready to slice and eat.
11. You will pull them off at 185-190°F internal temp in between the bones.

Pineapple-glazed Kurobuta Bone-in Ham With Bourbon-cherry Sauce

Servings:8
Cooking Time: 188 Minutes

Ingredients:
- 1 Snake River Farms American Kurobuta Half Bone-In Ham
- 1 pineapple, cut into ¼ inch rounds, marinated in ¼ cup bourbon for 4 hours (turn occasionally to keep the pineapple evenly coated)
- 2 cups pineapple juice

- ¼ cup bourbon
- 1 cup firmly packed dark brown sugar
- 1 tbsp cinnamon
- 1 tsp kosher salt
- 16 oz fresh cherries, pitted
- 1 cup pineapple juice
- ½ cup bourbon
- 2 tbsp unsalted butter
- 4 sprigs of thyme
- 1 tbsp balsamic glaze
- Salt to taste

Directions:

1. Preheat the grill to 325°F using direct heat with a cast iron grate installed.

2. Place the ham on the roasting rack and into the roasting pan. Place on the kamado grill and bake for 30 minutes. Glaze the ham with the pineapple glaze, reserving half. Bake for another 2 hours and coat with the remaining half of the glaze. Add the bourbon-soaked pineapple slices on top of the ham and secure with picks. Bake for another 30 minutes, or until the internal temperature is 155°F. Remove from the kamado grill and let rest for 10 minutes prior to slicing.

3. Remove the ham from the kamado grill and place on serving platter. Pour the leftover glaze from the roasting pan over the ham. Slice and serve the ham and top with the cherry sauce. Enjoy!

4. Preheat the grill to 325°F using direct heat with a cast iron grate installed.

5. In a small cast iron skillet, mix all of the ingredients for the glaze, place on the grid. Once the liquid starts to smoke, flambé the sauce using a long match (when you flambé, the bourbon flavor remains, the alcohol is removed, leaving most of the sugar behind). Continue cooking, stirring occasionally, until the liquid is reduced by half. Remove from the grill, carefully pour into a bowl and set aside.

6. 24-48 hours prior to cooking, soak the cherries in the bourbon in an airtight container, gently turning occasionally to keep the cherries evenly soaked.

7. In the dutch oven, mix all of the ingredients for the sauce, (including the bourbon the cherries soaked in). Place on the grid. Continue cooking until the liquid is reduced by half; this will take about as long as the ham is baking. Make sure to stir occasionally and add a small amount of water or pineapple juice if it thickens too quickly.

SIDES

Corn, Bacon & Chorizo Hash

Servings: 4
Cooking Time: 40 Minutes

Ingredients:

- 4 ears of corn, shucked
- 2 Fresno peppers
- 1lb (450g) new potatoes, halved if large
- 8oz (225g) chorizo sausage, casings removed
- 8oz (225g) thick-cut bacon, diced
- 2 shallots, finely diced
- kosher salt and freshly ground black pepper

Directions:

1. Preheat the grill to 350°F using indirect heat with a cast iron grate installed and a cast iron skillet on the grate. Place corn, peppers, and potatoes on the grate around the skillet, close the grill lid, and grill until beginning to soften and char, about 6 to 10 minutes. (Peppers and corn cook more quickly than the potatoes.) Remove the vegetables from the grill. Cut the kernels from the cobs, seed and dice the peppers, and dice the potatoes. Set aside.

2. In the hot skillet, cook chorizo for 10 minutes, stirring once or twice. Transfer the cooked chorizo to a platter and set aside. Return the skillet to the grill, add bacon, close the grill lid, and cook until crisp and the fat has rendered, about 10 minutes. Drain the bacon grease, reserving 1 tbsp in the skillet along with the cooked bacon, and return the skillet to the grill.

3. Add shallots to the skillet, close the grill lid, and sauté until soft and translucent, about 2 minutes. Add corn kernels, potatoes, and chorizo, close the grill lid, and sauté for 5 to 7 minutes more. Add half the diced peppers and season with salt and pepper. Taste to check the spice level before adding the remaining diced peppers. Stir and cook for 1 minute more. Remove the hash from the grill and serve immediately.

Cheesy Tomato Risotto

Servings: 6
Cooking Time: 35 Minutes

Ingredients:

- 1 tbsp unsalted butter
- 1/2 red onion, chopped
- 3 garlic cloves, minced
- 3/4 cup Arborio rice
- 3 cups chicken stock, warmed, plus more as needed
- 2 medium Roma tomatoes, diced small
- 2oz (55g) freshly shredded Parmesan cheese
- 2 scallions, thinly sliced
- 1 tbsp chopped fresh flat-leaf parsley

Directions:

1. Preheat the grill to 350ºF (177°C) using indirect heat with a standard grate installed and a dutch oven on the grate. In the hot dutch oven, melt butter. Add onion and garlic, close the grill lid, and cook until barely beginning to soften, about 2 minutes. Add rice, stir, and close the grill lid. Cook until rice is coated with butter and slightly toasted, about 2 to 3 minutes.

2. Add warm stock to the rice 1 cup at a time, stirring often. Add more stock only after the liquid from the previous addition is absorbed. (This will take about 10 minutes each time you add the liquid.) Add tomatoes and cheese, and stir until cheese melts. Add scallions and parsley, and stir until just combined. Remove the dutch oven from the grill and serve immediately.

Panzanella

Servings: 6
Cooking Time: 8 Minutes

Ingredients:

- 1/2 cup basil leaves
- 3 Tablespoons capers
- 2 large tomatoes, cut into 1 inch cubes
- 1 baguette, cut into 1 inch slices
- 1 yellow pepper, cut into 1 inch pieces
- 1 English cucumber, cut into 1 inch pieces
- 1/2 red onion, thinly sliced
- Olive oil
- Salt and Pepper
- 2 Tablespoons Dijon mustard
- 1/4 cup Champagne vinegar
- 1/2 cup olive oil
- 1/4 tsp salt
- 1/4 tsp pepper
- 2 cloves garlic, finely minced

Directions:

1. Brush the baguette slices with olive oil and place them on a 425°F grill.
2. Close the dome for 2 minutes, turn the bread, and close the dome for another 2-3 minutes or until the bread is golden brown.
3. Assembly:
4. Cut the toasted bread into 1 inch cubes and set aside.
5. In the bottom of a large bowl, combine dressing ingredients.
6. Add bread cubes, cucumber, tomato, bell pepper, and sliced onion and stir to combine.
7. Set aside at room temperature for 20 minutes before serving.

Grilled Artichokes

Servings: 4
Cooking Time: 7 Minutes

Ingredients:

- 4 large artichokes
- 2 Tablespoons olive oil
- 1 lemon
- Salt and pepper
- 1/2 cup mayonnaise
- 2 Tablespoons lemon juice
- 2 Tablespoons basil pesto
- 1/2 tsp sriracha

Directions:

1. Trim artichokes of their fibrous ends and thorny leaves.
2. Quarter the artichokes and remove the thistle in the middle.
3. Rub all cut ends with half of a lemon to prevent browning.
4. In a large steamer, cook artichokes 45 minutes or until just fork tender.
5. Brush each artichoke with olive oil and season with salt and pepper.
6. Grilling:
7. Preheat the grill to 425°F using direct heat with a cast iron grate installed and close the dome for 3 minutes.
8. Turn the artichokes and close the dome for another 2-4 minutes.
9. Serve with dipping sauce.

Potato, Squash, And Tomato Gratin

Servings: 8
Cooking Time: 35 Minutes

Ingredients:

- 1 lb Yukon gold potatoes, sliced 1/4 inch thick
- 1 lb yellow squash, sliced 1/4 inch thick

- 1/2 cup shredded parmesan cheese
- 5 tomatoes, sliced 1/4 inch thick
- 1/4 cup olive oil, divided
- 2 Tablespoons garlic, minced
- 1 tsp salt
- 1/2 tsp pepper

Directions:

1. Line the bottom of the dutch oven with 2 Tablespoon olive oil.

2. Layer potatoes on the bottom, topped with squash, and topped with tomatoes.

3. Season the tomatoes with salt, pepper, half of the garlic, and half of the parmesan cheese.

4. Repeat with remaining potatoes, squash, and tomatoes.

5. Season with salt, pepper, and remaining garlic.

6. Drizzle with remaining 2 Tablespoon of olive oil and top with remaining parmesan cheese.

7. Grilling:

8. Preheat the grill to 375°F using direct heat with a cast iron grate installed.

9. Place the dutch oven, uncovered, into the grill and close the dome for 30-35 minutes or until the potatoes are cooked through.

Roasted Potatoes

Servings: 20
Cooking Time: 30 Minutes

Ingredients:

- 2lb (1kg) fingerling potatoes, halved
- 1 tbsp chopped fresh cilantro
- 1 tbsp chopped fresh basil
- 1 tbsp chopped scallions, plus more to garnish
- 3 poblano peppers, diced
- 1/2 cup olive oil
- 1/2 cup white vinegar
- 3 garlic cloves, minced
- kosher salt and freshly ground black pepper
- 1 cup crumbled queso fresco

Directions:

1. Preheat the grill to 425°F (218°C) using indirect heat with a standard grate installed. In a dutch oven or a disposable aluminum baking dish, combine potatoes, cilantro, basil, scallions, peppers, oil, vinegar, and garlic. Toss well to ensure potatoes are coated in oil and seasonings. Place the dutch oven on the grate and cook until potatoes are fork tender, about 30 minutes.

2. Remove the dutch oven from the grill, season with salt and pepper to taste, and top with the queso fresco and more sliced scallions. Serve immediately.

Dutch Oven Baked Beans

Servings: 16
Cooking Time: 40 Minutes

Ingredients:

- 6 scallions, plus more to garnish
- 1lb (450g) bacon, diced
- 3 garlic cloves
- 4 x 15oz (420g) cans Great Northern beans
- 2 tbsp Chinese five-spice powder
- 1/2 cup chopped fresh cilantro
- 2 tbsp black bean garlic sauce
- 2 tsp ground ginger
- 3 tbsp soy sauce
- 1 cup sweet chili sauce

Directions:

1. Preheat the grill to 400°F (204°C) using indirect heat with a cast iron grate installed and a dutch oven on the grate. Place scallions on the grate around the dutch oven, close the grill lid, and grill until beginning to char, about 2 minutes. Chop scallions and set aside.

2. Place bacon in the dutch oven, close the grill lid, and cook until crisp, about 15 to 20 minutes, stirring occasionally. Use a slotted spoon to remove bacon from the dutch oven and set aside.

3. Drain all but 2 tbsp bacon fat from the dutch oven. Add scallions and garlic, close the grill lid, and cook until just fragrant, about 1 minute. Add beans, five-spice powder, cilantro, garlic sauce, ginger, soy sauce, and chili sauce, and stir to combine. Place the lid on the dutch oven, close the grill lid, and cook beans until heated through, about 15 minutes.

4. Remove the dutch oven from the grill, and stir bacon into the baked beans. Garnish with sliced scallions, and serve immediately.

Ratatouille

Servings: 4
Cooking Time: 30 Minutes

Ingredients:
- 1/2 cup fresh, shredded basil
- 2 cloves garlic, minced
- 2 large tomatoes, chopped
- 1 red bell pepper, chopped
- 1 large eggplant, peeled and cut into 1/2 inch cubes
- 1 onion, sliced thin
- 1/4 cup olive oil
- 1/4 tsp dried oregano
- 1/4 tsp dried thyme
- 1/4 tsp fennel seeds
- 3/4 tsp salt

Directions:
1. Preheat the grill to 350°F using direct heat with a cast iron grate installed with the dutch oven on the grid.
2. Add olive oil to the pot and toast oregano, thyme, and fennel for 1 minute.

3. Add onion and cook for 5 minutes or until the onion is soft.
4. Add remaining vegetables, cover, and lower the dome for 20-25 minutes.
5. Serve topped with basil.

Broiled Tomatoes And Parmesan

Servings: 4
Cooking Time: 5 Minutes

Ingredients:
- 1/4 cup parmesan, shredded
- 4 roma tomatoes
- 1 Tablespoon olive oil
- 1 tsp red wine vinegar
- Salt & Pepper

Directions:
1. Cut each tomato in half, lengthwise, and brush with olive oil.
2. Grilling:
3. Preheat the grill to 500°F using direct heat with a cast iron grate installed and lower the dome for 2 minutes.
4. Turn the tomatoes, season with vinegar, salt, and pepper and top with parmesan cheese.
5. Lower the dome for an additional 2 minutes or until the cheese melts. Serve warm.

Grilled Watermelon Salad

Servings: 6
Cooking Time: 6 Minutes

Ingredients:
- 4 medium cucumbers, about 1lb (450g) in total, divided
- 3lb (1.4kg) watermelon, rind removed and cut into thick slices
- 3 garlic cloves, peeled
- 1½ cups plain Greek yogurt

- 2/3 cup chopped mint, divided
- 3/4 tsp kosher salt
- 2 tbsp fresh lime juice
- flaky sea salt, to serve

Directions:

1. Preheat the grill to 500ºF (260°C) using direct heat with a cast iron grate installed. Peel 2 cucumbers and halve them lengthwise. Place the halved cucumbers and watermelon slices on the grate, close the lid, and grill until grill marks form, about 2 to 3 minutes per side.

2. Using a chef's knife, finely chop garlic and sprinkle with a pinch of salt. Using the flat of the blade, crush the chopped garlic, scrape into a pile, and crush again, repeating until a paste forms. Transfer to a medium bowl.

3. To make the tzatziki sauce, peel the remaining 2 cucumbers, halve lengthwise, and seed. Coarsely grate into the bowl with the garlic paste. Stir in yogurt, 1/3 cup mint, and salt.

4. Cut the watermelon into bite-sized pieces, and cut the grilled cucumber crosswise into 1/3-in (.75-cm) slices. Place cucumber and watermelon in a large bowl, toss with lime juice and the remaining 1/3 cup mint, and sprinkle with sea salt. Spoon the tzatziki sauce over top to serve.

Grilled Lemon Garlic Zucchini

Servings: 6
Cooking Time: 5 Minutes

Ingredients:

- 4 zucchini, sliced lengthwise into 1/2 inch slices
- 1/4 cup butter, softened
- 2 tsp parsley, chopped
- 3 cloves garlic, minced
- The zest and juice of 1 lemon

Directions:

1. In a small dish, combine butter, parsley, garlic, lemon zest, and lemon juice.

2. Liberally brush each zucchini slice with the butter mixture.

3. Grilling:

4. Place the zucchini on a 500°F grill and close the dome for 3 minutes.

5. Flip the zucchini and recover with the dome for an additional 2 minutes.

6. Drizzle remaining butter on top of zucchini as it comes off the grill. Serve warm.

Wood-plank Loaded Mashed Potatoes

Servings: 16
Cooking Time: 50 Minutes

Ingredients:

- 1lb (450g) red potatoes
- 1lb (450g) Yukon Gold potatoes
- 1 tbsp kosher salt, plus 1 tsp
- 2 strips bacon, diced
- 2 tbsp unsalted butter
- 1/4 cup sour cream
- 1/4 cup heavy cream
- 4oz (113g) shredded Cheddar cheese, plus more for topping
- 4 scallions, thinly sliced, plus more for topping
- freshly ground black pepper

Directions:

1. Place a 4 x 9in (10 x 23cm) cedar wood plank in a baking dish, cover with cold water, and place heavy cans or stones on the plank to keep it submerged. Soak for 1 to 2 hours.

2. Place red potatoes and Yukon Gold potatoes in a large stockpot and add cold water to cover by

several inches. Place the pot on the stovetop over high heat, add 1 tsp salt, and bring to a boil. Reduce to a simmer, cover, and cook until potatoes are fork tender, about 25 minutes. Drain potatoes, reserving 1 cup cooking water.

3. Preheat the grill to 350°F (177°C) using direct heat with a standard grate installed and a cast iron skillet on the grate. Add bacon to the hot skillet, and cook until bacon is crisp and the fat has rendered, about 10 to 15 minutes, stirring occasionally. Transfer the cooked bacon pieces to a plate lined with a paper towel.

4. In a large bowl, combine potatoes, butter, sour cream, heavy cream, Cheddar cheese, scallions, bacon, and 1 tbsp salt. Mash with a potato masher until potatoes have broken down and cheese and sour cream are fully incorporated. If potatoes are too stiff, add some of the reserved cooking water.

5. Place the soaked plank on the grate and allow it to heat for 2 to 5 minutes, then flip it over. Scoop the mashed potatoes onto the heated side of the plank. Top the potatoes with a little Cheddar cheese, close the lid, and cook until cheese has melted and potatoes have browned slightly, about 7 to 10 minutes. Remove potatoes from the grill, sprinkle with scallions, and serve immediately.

Smoked Potato Salad

Servings: 8
Cooking Time: 120 Minutes

Ingredients:

- 4 large baking potatoes
- 4 large eggs, hard boiled and finely chopped
- 2 green onions, finely chopped
- 2 large dill pickles, finely chopped
- 1 rib celery, finely diced
- 1/2 cup mayonnaise
- The juice of 1 lemon
- 1/2 tsp black pepper
- 1/2 tsp celery seed
- 1/2 tsp dried dill

Directions:

1. Scrub the potatoes.
2. Grilling:
3. Place the potatoes alongside meat that is smoking at 225°F.
4. Assembly:
5. When the potatoes are fork tender, chill in the refrigerator for 30 minutes.
6. Peel and cut potatoes into small cubes.
7. In a large bowl, combine dressing ingredients.
8. Add potatoes, eggs, green onion, pickle, and celery to the dressing and gently toss

Corn & Tomato Salsa

Servings: 8
Cooking Time: 10 Minutes

Ingredients:

- 6 ears of corn, shucked
- 1 lime, halved
- 1 avocado, halved
- 1lb (450g) grape tomatoes, quartered
- 1/2 tsp kosher salt, plus more as needed
- 1/2 tsp ground black pepper, plus more as needed
- 2 tsp olive oil
- 4oz (110g) blue cheese, crumbled
- 10 fresh basil leaves, sliced

Directions:

1. Preheat the grill to 425°F (218°C) using direct heat with a cast iron grate installed. Place corn, avocado, and lime on the grate, close the lid, and grill until beginning to soften and char, about 7 to 10 minutes. Transfer the corn, avocado, and

lime to a cutting board. Cut the kernels from the corn and dice the avocado.

2. In a large bowl, gently combine corn, tomatoes, avocado, salt, and pepper. Squeeze the grilled lime over top, drizzle with olive oil, and toss to coat.

3. Top the corn mixture with blue cheese and basil, and toss one final time. Season with salt and pepper to taste. Serve immediately.

Grilled Caesar Salad

Servings: 6
Cooking Time: 1 Minutes

Ingredients:

- 2 Tablespoons shredded Parmesan cheese
- 1 Tablespoon olive oil
- 1/4 tsp salt
- 2 heads romaine lettuce, split lengthwise
- 1 cup grated Parmesan cheese
- 2 Tablespoons Dijon mustard
- 3 garlic cloves
- 3 anchovy fillets
- 2 lemons, juiced
- Extra-virgin olive oil
- Kosher salt
- 2 Tablespoons olive oil
- 4 slices day old Italian bread, cubed
- Kosher Salt & Black Pepper to taste

Directions:

1. In a blender or food processor, combine dressing ingredients, minus olive oil and salt.

2. Gradually stream in olive oil until the dressing reaches your desired consistency.

3. Taste and season with salt, if necessary.

4. Grilling:

5. Preheat the grill to 400°F using direct heat with a cast iron grate installed.

6. Toss bread cubes with olive oil, a pinch of salt and a pinch of black pepper and place on a small sheet tray.

7. Place the bread in the grill for 8-10 minutes or until golden brown.

8. Brush cut side of the romaine halves with olive oil and season with salt and pepper.

9. Grill 1 minute over direct heat.

10. Cut the romaine into bite size pieces.

11. Toss lettuce with dressing, croutons, and shredded Parmesan Serve immediately.

Sweet Potato Bake

Servings: 6
Cooking Time: 20 Minutes

Ingredients:

- 3 cups cooked and mashed sweet potatoes, cooled
- 1/2 cup butter, melted
- 1/2 cup sugar
- 1/2 cup milk
- 1 tsp vanilla extract
- 1/2 tsp salt
- 3 eggs, beaten
- 1 cup brown sugar
- 1/2 cup self-rising flour
- 1 cup chopped pecans
- 4 Tablespoons butter at room temperature

Directions:

1. Line the dutch oven with a liner.

2. In a large bowl, combine souffle ingredients. Pour into the prepared dutch oven.

3. In a separate small bowl, combine brown sugar, self-rising flour, chopped pecans, and room temperature butter until a crumbly mixture forms.

4. Sprinkle the crumb mixture over the sweet potato mixture.

5. Grilling:

6. Preheat the grill to 400°F using direct heat with a cast iron grate installed.

7. Place the dutch oven, uncovered, into the grill for 20-25 minutes or until the top is golden brown.

Corn & Poblano Pudding

Servings: 8
Cooking Time: 30 Minutes

Ingredients:

- vegetable oil, for greasing
- 4 ears of sweet corn, shucked
- 1 poblano pepper, left whole
- 4 large eggs
- 1 cup whole milk
- 1⁄2 tsp kosher salt
- 1⁄4 tsp ground nutmeg
- 1⁄4 tsp ground cayenne pepper
- 2oz (55g) shredded Cheddar cheese

Directions:

1. Preheat the grill to 350°F (177°C) using indirect heat with a standard grate installed. Grease a cast iron skillet with oil.

2. Place corn and pepper on the grate, positioning them around the edges, close the lid, and grill until beginning to soften and char, about 10 minutes. Transfer the vegetables to a cutting board, cut the kernels from the cobs, and seed and dice the pepper.

3. In a large bowl, whisk together eggs, milk, salt, nutmeg, cayenne, and cheese until well combined. Stir in corn kernels and pepper. Pour the mixture into the greased dish and place on the grate. Close the lid and bake until a knife inserted halfway between the center and the outer edge comes out clean, about 20 minutes.

Remove the pudding from the grill and serve warm or at room temperature.

Prosciutto And Pear Bruschetta

Servings: 6
Cooking Time: 5 Minutes

Ingredients:

- 4 oz prosciutto
- 4 oz shaved parmesan cheese
- 1 cup baby arugula
- 1 baguette, sliced 1/2 inch thick
- 1 pear, sliced thin
- 2 Tablespoons olive oil
- 2 Tablespoons high quality balsamic vinegar

Directions:

1. Brush each baguette slice with olive oil and place on a 325°F grill with the dome closed for 5 minutes.

2. Assembly:

3. Remove bread slices and top each with prosciutto, pear slices, parmesan, and baby arugula.

4. Drizzle a few drops of balsamic vinegar over each bruschetta and serve.

Mexican Street Corn

Servings: 6
Cooking Time: 10 Minutes

Ingredients:

- 6 ears corn
- 1/2 cup cotija cheese
- 1 Tablespoon chili powder
- 1 cup mayonnaise
- 1 lime, cut into wedges

Directions:

1. Pull back the husk of the corn and thoroughly remove the silk from each ear of corn.

2. Soak the corn in water for 20 minutes before cooking.

3. Peel back the husks to reveal the corn.

4. Grilling:

5. Preheat the grill to 450°F using direct heat with a cast iron grate installed.

6. Close the dome for 5 minutes, turn the corn, and close the dome for an additional 5 minutes.

7. Remove the corn from the grill. Spread with mayonnaise, sprinkle with chili powder, and coat with cotija cheese.

8. Serve with lime wedges.

Soba Noodle Bowl

Servings: 6
Cooking Time: 30 Minutes

Ingredients:
- 12oz (28g) soba noodles
- 4 scallions
- 2 red bell peppers, left whole
- 1 carrot, peeled
- 1/2 head of napa cabbage
- 1/4 cup chopped hazelnuts
- chopped fresh cilantro, to garnish
- for the sauce
- 1/2 cup peanut butter
- 1/4 cup soy sauce
- 1/3 cup warm water
- 2 tbsp ground ginger
- 1 garlic clove
- 2 tbsp white wine vinegar
- 11/2 tsp honey
- 1 tsp crushed red pepper flakes

Directions:
1. To make the sauce, combine all the sauce ingredients in a blender and purée until smooth. Set aside. (Sauce can be made in advance.

Refrigerate in an airtight container and use within 1 week.)

2. Cook the pasta according to the package directions until cooked but still firm to the bite. Drain and rinse well under cold water. Set aside.

3. Preheat the grill to 400°F (204°C) using direct heat with a cast iron grate installed and a cast iron skillet on the grate. Place scallions, peppers, carrot, and napa cabbage around the skillet, close the lid, and grill until beginning to soften and char, about 7 to 10 minutes. Slice peppers and carrots thinly, and shred cabbage.

4. Add the vegetables and noodles to the hot skillet, and stir to combine. Add the sauce, and stir until well incorporated and heated through, about 3 to 4 minutes.

5. Remove the skillet from the grill and top noodles with hazelnuts and cilantro. Serve immediately.

Baba Ganoush

Servings: 8
Cooking Time: 10 Minutes

Ingredients:
- 2 Tablespoons fresh parsley
- 1 eggplant, sliced into 1/2 inch rounds
- 1 clove garlic
- The juice and zest of 1 lemon
- 2 Tablespoons olive oil
- 2 Tablespoons tahini
- Salt & Pepper

Directions:
1. Brush both sides of each eggplant slice with olive oil and season with salt and pepper.

2. Preheat the grill to 425°F using direct heat with a cast iron grate installed and close the dome for 3-5 minutes.

3. Flip the eggplant and close the dome for another 3-5 minutes.

4. Assembly:

5. Peel the eggplant skins away from the flesh and discard.

6. In a food processor, combine eggplant, tahini, parsley, garlic, lemon zest and lemon juice and puree until smooth.

7. Taste for seasoning and add salt and pepper accordingly.

8. Serve at room temperature with pita chips, pretzels, or raw vegetables.

Cowboy Caviar

Servings: 8
Cooking Time: 10 Minutes

Ingredients:
- 2 ears fresh corn on the cob
- 1 large tomato, finely diced
- 1 bell pepper, finely diced
- 1 jalapeño, very finely chopped
- 1/4 cup bottled Italian salad dressing
- 2 cans black beans, drained and rinsed
- 1 can pinto beans, drained and rinsed

Directions:
1. Place shucked and cleaned ears of corn on a 425°F grill and close the dome for 5 minutes.

2. Turn the corn and close the dome for another 5 minutes before removing and setting aside.

3. Assembly:

4. Carefully cut the corn off the cob and place it in a large bow.

5. Add remaining ingredients and toss to combine.

Summer Squash & Eggplant

Servings: 6
Cooking Time: 35 Minutes

Ingredients:
- 1 medium yellow squash
- 2 medium zucchini
- 1/4 cup olive oil
- 2 medium yellow onions, sliced into half moons
- 1 medium eggplant, peeled and cut into cubes
- 2 garlic cloves, minced
- 1/2 tsp dried oregano
- 2 cups dry white wine, such as Chardonnay
- 4 tbsp unsalted butter
- kosher salt and freshly ground black pepper
- lemon slices, to serve (optional)

Directions:
1. Preheat the grill to 425°F (218°C) using direct heat with a cast iron grate installed and a dutch oven on the grate. Place squash and zucchini on the grate around the dutch oven, close the lid, and grill until beginning to soften and char, about 5 to 7 minutes. Remove vegetables from the grill and slice into rounds.

2. In the hot dutch oven, heat oil until shimmering. Add onions, and sauté until translucent, about 7 to 8 minutes. Add squash, zucchini, eggplant, garlic, and oregano. Close the lid and sauté until vegetables begin to soften, about 15 minutes. Add white wine, close the grill lid, and simmer until the vegetables have begun to soften and the liquid has reduced by half, about 5 minutes.

3. Remove the dutch oven from the grill and add the butter, stirring until melted. Season well with salt and pepper and a squeeze of lemon. Serve hot with lemon slices (if using).

Campfire Potato Salad

Servings: 10

Cooking Time: 10 Minutes

Ingredients:

- 2lb (1kg) new potatoes, unpeeled
- 1 green bell pepper, left whole
- 1 red bell pepper, left whole
- 1/2 red onion
- 1/4 cup mayonnaise
- 1/4 cup sour cream
- 1 tbsp Dijon mustard
- 3/4 tsp garlic, minced
- 1 tbsp kosher salt
- 1/4 tsp ground black pepper
- 1 tbsp chopped fresh dill
- 2 celery stalks, diced

Directions:

1. Preheat the grill to 425°F (218°C) using direct heat with a cast iron grate installed. Place potatoes, peppers, and onion on the grate, close the lid, and grill until beginning to soften and char, about 7 to 10 minutes, turning once or twice.

2. Remove the vegetables from the grill and let cool slightly. Cut the potatoes into quarters and dice the peppers and onion.

3. In a large bowl, combine mayonnaise, sour cream, mustard, garlic, salt, pepper, and dill. Add potatoes, peppers, onions, and celery to the mayonnaise mixture, and gently combine until the vegetables are evenly coated with the dressing. Taste and adjust the seasoning as needed. Serve warm.

Sweet Potato Fries

Servings: 4

Cooking Time: 25 Minutes

Ingredients:

- 1 tsp fresh thyme, chopped
- 4 large sweet potatoes
- 4 cloves garlic, minced
- 1/4 cup olive oil
- Salt and Pepper

Directions:

1. In a large pot, cover sweet potatoes with cold water and add 2 tsp salt.

2. Bring the water to a boil and cook until the potatoes are soft, but firm, about 15 minutes.

3. In a small sauce pan, heat 2 Tablespoon of the olive oil, garlic, and thyme until fragrant.

4. Cut each sweet potato in half, lengthwise, then in 3 or 4 spears.

5. Brush each spear on cut sides with olive oil, season with salt and pepper.

6. Grilling:

7. Preheat the grill to 425°F using direct heat with a cast iron grate installed and close the dome for 3 minutes.

8. Turn the potatoes and close the dome for an additional 3 minutes or until the sweet potatoes have finished cooking through.

9. Remove the fries and toss with the garlic and thyme oil before serving.

Mac And Cheese

Servings: 6

Cooking Time: 60 Minutes

Ingredients:

- 1 lb smoked cheddar cheese, shredded, divided
- 1/4 cup butter
- 2 eggs
- 1/2 lb elbow macaroni
- 3/4 cups evaporated milk
- 1/4 cup Panko breadcrumbs

- 1 tsp salt
- 3/4 tsp dry mustard

Directions:

1. In a large pot of boiling, salted water cook the macaroni according to package directions and drain.

2. In a separate bowl, whisk together the eggs, milk, hot sauce, salt, pepper, and mustard.

3. Grilling:

4. Preheat the grill to 350°F using direct heat with a cast iron grate installed with the dutch oven on the grid.

5. Melt the butter in the dutch oven and place macaroni in the pot. Toss to coat.

6. Stir the egg and milk mixture into the pasta and add half of the cheese.

7. Continuously stir the mac and cheese for 3 minutes or until creamy.

8. Top with remaining cheese and Panko breadcrumbs.

9. Cover the dutch oven, lower the dome, and cook for 20-25 minutes.

10. Serve immediately.

Wood-plank Stuffed Tomatoes

Servings: 8
Cooking Time: 20 Minutes

Ingredients:

- 4 beefsteak tomatoes
- 1 cup chopped fresh flat-leaf parsley
- 3/4 cup Italian-style breadcrumbs
- 1 cup grated provolone
- 1/4 tsp ground black pepper
- 1 tsp unsalted butter, softened
- 2 tbsp extra virgin olive oil

Directions:

1. Place a 4 x 9in (10 x 23cm) wood plank in a baking dish, cover with cold water, and place heavy cans or stones on the plank to keep it submerged. Soak for 1 to 2 hours.

2. Preheat the grill to 425°F (218°C) using indirect heat with a standard grate installed. Place the wood plank on the grate.

3. Cut tomatoes in half horizontally and hollow out the insides, discarding the seeds and reserving the pulp. Chop the reserved pulp and place in a medium bowl. Add parsley, breadcrumbs, provolone, and pepper, and mix gently to combine. Fill each tomato half with the breadcrumb mixture and top with a drizzle of oil.

4. Flip the plank over, spread butter on the hot side, and arrange tomatoes cut side up on the plank. Place the plank on the grate, close the lid, and cook until the tops are browned and the tomatoes are soft, about 20 minutes. Remove tomatoes from the grill and serve immediately.

Alligator Eggs

Servings: 6
Cooking Time: 10 Minutes

Ingredients:

- 8 ounces cream cheese, softened
- 1 cup sharp cheddar cheese
- 12 thin slices bacon
- 6 jalapeños

Directions:

1. Slice jalapeños in half and remove seeds. Set aside.

2. In a small bowl, combine cheddar cheese and cream cheese until mixed.

3. Stuff 2 Tablespoon of the cream cheese mixture into each jalapeño half.

4. Wrap each jalapeño half in one strip of bacon, securing with a toothpick.

5. Grilling:

6. Preheat the grill to 425°F using direct heat with a cast iron grate installed.

7. Place the alligator eggs directly on the grid and close the dome for 10 minutes or until the bacon is crisp. Serve immediately.

German Potato Salad

Servings: 8
Cooking Time: 70 Minutes

Ingredients:
- 2lb (1kg) Yukon Gold potatoes, unpeeled and cut into rounds or bite-sized pieces
- 1/2lb (225g) thick-cut bacon
- 3/4 cup finely chopped yellow onion
- 1/3 cup white vinegar
- 1/4 cup sugar
- 1 tbsp Dijon mustard
- 1 tsp kosher salt
- 2 tbsp minced chives, to garnish

Directions:
1. Preheat the grill to 350ºF (177°C) using indirect heat with a cast iron grate installed and a cast iron skillet on the grate. Place potatoes on the grate around the skillet, close the lid, and roast until fork tender, about 45 minutes. Remove potatoes from the grill and set aside.

2. Add bacon to the hot skillet, close the lid, and cook until crisp, about 10 to 15 minutes. Once crisp, transfer to a plate lined with a paper towel and crumble into small pieces. Pour off the rendered fat, reserving 4 tbsp in the skillet.

3. Add onion to the skillet, close the lid, and cook until translucent and beginning to brown, about 4 to 5 minutes. Whisk in vinegar, sugar, mustard, and salt, and stir until thick and bubbly, about 2 to 3 minutes. Add the cooked potatoes, and toss to coat.

4. Remove the skillet from the grill, top with crumbled bacon, and garnish with chives. Serve warm.

Grilled Paneer

Servings: 6
Cooking Time: 30 Minutes

Ingredients:
- 4 tbsp unsalted butter
- 1 medium white onion, diced
- 3 tbsp chopped fresh ginger
- 1 jalapeño pepper, diced
- 1 tbsp vindaloo curry powder
- 1 tsp kosher salt, divided
- 28oz (800g) can whole peeled tomatoes, preferably fire roasted
- 1/2 tsp ground cinnamon
- 2 tbsp crushed lime leaves
- 3 tbsp honey
- 1/2 cup heavy cream
- 1lb (450g) paneer cheese, thickly sliced
- 8oz (225g) arugula
- 1/4 cup chopped fresh cilantro
- naan bread, to serve (optional)

Directions:
1. Preheat the grill to 425°F (218°C) using direct heat with a cast iron grate installed and cast iron skillet or an all-metal saucepan on the grate. Once hot, add butter to the skillet, stirring until melted, then stir in onion, ginger, and jalapeño.

Sprinkle curry powder and 1/2 tsp salt over top and cook until onions begin to soften and brown, about 5 to 7 minutes, stirring occasionally.

2. Add tomatoes, cinnamon, lime leaves, and honey, pressing tomatoes with a wooden spoon to break them down. Cook uncovered until the sauce thickens and only a little liquid remains, about10 to 15 minutes, stirring occasionally.

3. Transfer the sauce to a blender (or use an immersion blender), and purée on high speed a until smooth, about 1 minute. Wipe the skillet clean and return to the grill. Pour the sauce through a fine mesh strainer back into the skillet. Stir in cream and the remaining 1/2 tsp salt, adding more of each to taste.

4. Place paneer on the grate, close the lid, and cook until the cheese has visible grill marks, about 2 to 3 minutes per side. Cut into large cubes and add to the curry sauce. Gently stir in arugula and half the cilantro. Sprinkle the remaining cilantro over top, and serve immediately with warmed naan (if desired).

RECIPE INDEX

"the Masterpiece" 84
3 Ingredient Fruit Cobbler 51
4 Ingredient, No Knead Bread 50

A
Adobo Chicken Wings 93
Aged Prime Rib 64
Alligator Eggs 118
Almond Cream Cake 56
Amusement Park Turkey Legs 42
Apple Cinnamon Pork Chops 102
Apple Pizza 53
Asian Beef & Mushroom Tacos 67

B
Baba Ganoush 115
Baby Back Ribs With Quince Barbecue Sauce 89
Bacon Cheeseburger Hotdogs 69
Bacon Mac & Cheese 90
Bacon Roses 86
Bacon-wrapped Bbq Quail 32
Baked Brie With Chutney And Crisp Bacon 15
Banana Boats 57
Barbecue Chicken With Alabama White Sauce 34
Beef Asparagus Stir Fry 72
Beer-infused Baby Back Ribs 98
Berry Upside-down Cake 49
Best Banana Bread 54
Blackened Grouper 15
Blue Cheese Compound Butter Grilled Oysters 14
Bou Lentil Turkey Burgers 43
Bourbon-glazed Cold Smoked Salmon 25
Braised Carnitas With Chimichurri Sauce 100
Breakfast Burger 82

Brined Roasted Turkey 39
Brisket Burnt Ends 63
Broiled Tomatoes And Parmesan 110
Brownies 48
Brunswick Stew 92
Buttermilk Biscuits 59

C
Cajun Shrimp Burgers 23
Campfire Potato Salad 117
Caramel Cinnamon Rolls 48
Carolina Pulled Pork 101
Cedar Planked Honey Glazed Salmon With Grilled Lemon Butter Asparagus 26
Champagne Quail 32
Championship Ribs 88
Charlotte Pork Chops 103
Cheesy Tomato Risotto 107
Chicken & Dumplings 44
Chicken And Shrimp Paella 14
Chile Rubbed Grilled Pork Chops 87
Chili Crusted Boar Ham 98
Chocolate Cake 51
Chocolate Chip Cookie Peanut Butter Cup S'mores 53
Cigar Dave's Alpha-meal 28
Cioppino (chip-ee-no) 28
Classic American Burger 82
Cold-smoked Rock Shrimp 22
Corn & Jalapeño Focaccia 59
Corn & Poblano Pudding 114
Corn & Tomato Salsa 112
Corn, Bacon & Chorizo Hash 107
Country Chicken Saltimbocca 46
Country Christmas 94
Cowboy Caviar 116
Crab Quiche 29

Cranberry-marinated Rack Of Lamb 63
Cuban Chicken Bombs 33
Cuban Pork (lechon Asado) 96

D
Death By Chocolate 51
Dutch Oven Baked Beans 109

F
Famous Dave's Five Star Bbq Sticky Ribs 97
Fire Grilled Steak With Steakhouse Butter 66
Fish And Shrimp Stuffed Jalapeños 16
Fish Tacos 18
Foil Packet Fish Filets 22
Fresh Peach Crisp 53
Fresh Smoked Bacon 87

G
Garfunkel Chicken 30
German Potato Salad 119
Ginger Garlic Shrimp Stir-fry 24
Greg Bates Bbq Chicken 42
Grill Glazed Sweet Asian Chicken Pan Grill 43
Grilled Artichokes 108
Grilled Asian Mahi-mahi 27
Grilled Buffalo Steaks 79
Grilled Caesar Salad 113
Grilled Chicken Fajita Skewers 41
Grilled Duck Breast With Apple Brandy Glaze 31
Grilled Fish Tacos 27
Grilled Lemon Garlic Zucchini 111
Grilled Lobster 21
Grilled Naan 61
Grilled Paneer 119
Grilled Pineapple Sundaes 54
Grilled Plums With Honey And Ricotta 48
Grilled Salmon 13
Grilled Shrimp And Linguica Skewers 16

Grilled Shrimp Cocktail With Fire-roasted Cocktail Sauce 13
Grilled Shrimp, Romaine And Avocado Salad 28
Grilled Sopapillas 50
Grilled Top Blade Steak 68
Grilled Watermelon Salad 110
Grilled Watermelon With Honey Yogurt 54

H
Hatch Chile Salsa And Chicken Casserole 34
Herb-crusted Pork Short Ribs 102
Herbed-up Prime Rib 80
Hoisin Glazed Wings 45
Honey Pork Tenderloin Kabob 94
Hop's Hawaiian Bbq Chicken Pizza 38

K
Korean Short Ribs 81
Korean-style Beef Short Ribs 72

L
Lamb Shawarma 40
Lemon Pepper Wings 30
Lemon Poppy Seed Cake 60
Lemon Scented Chicken Thighs 33
London Bridge London Broil 74

M
Mac And Cheese 117
Mediterranean Surf And Turf Kabobs 25
Mexican Street Corn 114

N
Nutella And Strawberry Pizza 62
Ny Strip Steaks 75

O
O'neill Williams' Turkey Parmesan 33
Oahu Burger 83
Open-faced Leftover Turkey Sandwich 37
Orange Scented Vanilla Cake 53

Oyster Spaghetti 19
Oysters On The Half Shell 17

P

Panzanella 108
Pastrami Beef Short Ribs 76
Peach Dutch Baby 52
Peaches And Pound Cake 55
Peanut Butter Bacon Bars 57
Peking Duck 45
Pig Candy 99
Pimento Cheese Burger With Bacon Jam 80
Pineapple-glazed Kurobuta Bone-in Ham With
Bourbon-cherry Sauce 105
Pizza Margherita 61
Polynesian Duck Kabobs 36
Porchetta 91
Pork Cacciatore 103
Potato, Squash, And Tomato Gratin 108
Prosciutto And Pear Bruschetta 114
Prosciutto Wrapped Cheese Dogs 94
Pulled Lamb Nachos 74

Q

Quesadilla Burger 83

R

Ratatouille 110
Ray's At Killer Creek's Short Ribs 71
Ray's Herb Butter Prime Rib 78
Red Gold Spicy Burgers 68
Reuben Riffel's Yellow Bellied Pork 85
Reverse-sear Ribeye 78
Roasted Halibut With Greek Relish 24
Roasted Potatoes 109
Rosemary Grilled Chicken Sandwiches 36
Round Roast Cheesesteaks With Pepper Jack
Cheese Sauce 73

S

S'mores Pizza 57

Savory Beer Can Chicken 41
Scallops, Asparagus And Artichoke Gratin 21
Seared Bison Filet 68
Seared Scallops 17
Seasonal Fruit Cobbler 60
Short Ribs & Polenta 70
Shrimp And Grits Kabobs 20
Smoked Andouille & Crawfish Gumbo 91
Smoked Beef Birria 66
Smoked Beef Brisket 73
Smoked Beef Short Ribs 65
Smoked Bourbon Chili 77
Smoked Chicken Wings 30
Smoked Oxtail Stew 67
Smoked Planked Trout 18
Smoked Pork Loin Sandwich 85
Smoked Potato Salad 112
Smoked Wings With Moonshine White Sauce
And Ranch Pickles 32
Smoky Grilled Chicken Nachos 40
Smoky Thai Pulled Chicken Sandwiches 37
Soba Noodle Bowl 115
Sourdough Baguette 58
Spicy Bbq Spare Ribs 99
Sriracha Pork Chops 96
Steakhouse Meatballs With French Fries And
Tzatziki Sauce 71
Stir-fried Cucumber And Pork With Golden
Garlic 88
Stir-fry Szechuan Beef 77
Stuffed Pork Chops With Poblano Cream
Sauce 104
Summer Squash & Eggplant 116
Sweet Potato Bake 113
Sweet Potato Fries 117
Swordfish Steaks With Peach Salsa 19

T

Taco Soup 79

Takeo Spikes' Ribs 104
The Crowned Jewels Burger 83
Triple Berry Crostata 55
Tuna Kabobs 18

U

Ultimate Bacon Jam Burger 75
Upside Down Triple Berry Pie 49

V

Vidalia Onion And Sriracha-glazed Nashville
Hot Wings 35

W

Watermelon Pizza 22
Whole Apples With Caramel Sauce 56
Whole Smoked Barbecue Chicken 39
Wild Rice Turkey Biryani Stuffed Whole
Pumpkin 44
Wood-plank Loaded Mashed Potatoes 111
Wood-plank Stuffed Tomatoes 118